yes I said
yes I will
Yes.

yes I said yes I will Yes.

A Celebration of James Joyce, *Ulysses*, and 100 Years of Bloomsday

Foreword by Frank McCourt
Introduction by Isaiah Sheffer
Edited by Nola Tully

VINTAGE BOOKS

A DIVISION OF RANDOM HOUSE, INC.

NEW YORK

Map Index

* Sites marked with an asterisk are outside the area of this map.

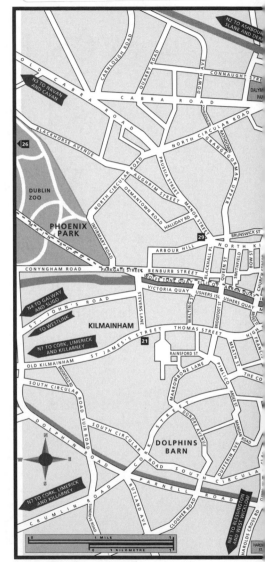

The site of Leopold Bloom's house at 7 Eccles Street (No. 4) is now marked by a plaque. The front door is preserved nearby in the James Joyce Centre at 35 North Great Georges Street, where exhibitions, tours and other Joycean activities take place.

James Joyce's Dublin:
In the Footsteps of Leopold Bloom

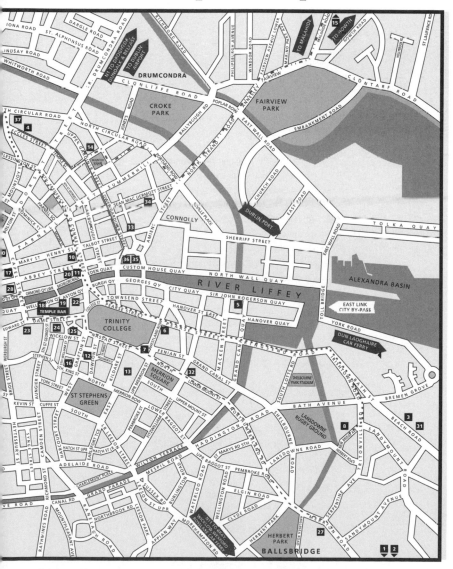

Bloom's lunchtime route through the city center is marked by a series of fourteen bronze pavement plaques running from the *Evening Telegraph* office (No. 10) to the National Museum (beside the National Library at No. 13). The plaques were laid in 1988 as part of the Dublin Millennium celebrations.

A VINTAGE BOOKS ORIGINAL, APRIL 2004

Foreword © 2004 by Frank McCourt
Introduction © 2004 by Isaiah Sheffer
Running text © 2004 by Nola Tully
"James Joyce and Neuchâtel" © 2004 by Lettie Teague
"*Ulysses*, Bloomsday, and Copyright" © 2004 by Robert Spoo
"A Handwritten Odyssey: Joyce's Manuscripts" © 2004 by Michael Barsanti
"Yes I Said: Translating *Ulysses* into Chinese" © 2004 by Jin Di
"*Ulysses* Without Tears: Teaching the Young a Difficult Book" © 2004 by Mary Gordon
Compilation © 2004 by Sideshow Media LLC

Vintage and colophon are registered trademarks of Random House, Inc.

The Cataloging-in-Publication Data is on file at the Library of Congress.

Vintage ISBN: 1-4000-7731-1

Book produced by Sideshow Media LLC

Editorial director and project manager: Dan Tucker
Designer: Elizabeth Zimmermann
Editorial assistant: Sarah Kramer

www.vintagebooks.com

Printed in the United States of America

10 9 8 7 6 5 4 3 2 1

Contents

Foreword

Frank McCourt

The title of the thesis I wrote at Brooklyn College in May 1964 was "Oliver St. John Gogarty: A Critical Study." Critical, my arse. I was no more qualified to write a critical study of Gogarty than I was to drive an eighteen-wheeler in a New York City rush hour. But the professors accepted it (some admired it) and here it is before me. Here, bristling with footnotes and backed up, not merely with one thirty-one-item bibliography, but also with a supplementary bibliography to show I knew my way around Catullus and Horace and Petronius and could show how indebted Gogarty was to them, how he often imitated them.

If you're holding this book in your hands you must know that Oliver St. John Gogarty was, for a while, a pal of James Joyce. You'll know how they knocked around together, Gogarty roistering, Joyce watching, watching, and making notes.

The thesis opens with a quote from Gogarty's *It Isn't This Time of Year at All:*

> It is with the unruly, the formless, the growing and illogical I love to deal. Even my gargoyles are merry and bright; my outer darkness by terror is unthronged. My thoughts are subjected to no rules. Behold the wings upon my helmet and my unfettered feet. I can fly backwards and forwards in time and space.

My comment on the above was, "The words are carefree, heroic and joyous. They come from the pen of Oliver St. John Gogarty, surgeon, poet, athlete, wit, senator, aviator, and close friend of great Irish literary figures."

What I omitted in this catalogue of Gogarty's activities and talents was his friendship with the man who made him immortal, James Joyce. It was an immortality Gogarty did not relish, an immortality that plunged him into a resentment of Joyce from which he never emerged.

You are now wondering: Why is this man going on about Gogarty when it's Joyce we're concerned with here?

Here is the answer: I wrote my thesis on Gogarty because I admired him, his diversity, his talents, his devil-may-care attitude toward life. If offered the chance for another life, I would ask to be reincarnated as Oliver St. John Gogarty.

I could have attempted a thesis on Joyce but the world was already busy with a thousand such tomes. So...I saw Gogarty as the next best thing, a door to the work, the mind, the life of The Master.

Nineteen sixty-four, the year of my forgettable thesis, was the sixtieth anniversary of Bloomsday. (Richard Ellmann had published his masterly biography in 1959.) Joyceans might have marked June 16 on their calendars in 1964 but you'd search in vain for the kind of celebration the day has engendered since. In certain places *Ulysses*, all of it, is read by people, some who haven't the foggiest notion of what they're reading. Still, the book sings in your head for a long time and you won't forget its characters—Bloom, Stephen, Molly, Blazes Boylan, or scenes. It's your life.

At these readings there is still a thrill in the crowd with the opening line that Joyceans know refers to my man, Gogarty: "Stately, plump Buck Mulligan came from the stairhead...." We're off on a journey through Dublin and Ireland and family and Catholicism and eroticism and love and infidelity. The journey ends on a powerful, tumescent note, "yes I will Yes." (Note the uppercase Y on the final *Yes*. This is not an end but a beginning.)

Let us digress a bit here. Joyce won't mind and I'm sure you won't.

Here is a strange fact: Neither Joyce nor Proust ever won the Nobel Prize. Wags have suggested they were ignored because the members of the Nobel Literature Committee were incapable of reading their work.

Another fact: According to the American publisher, Random House, *Ulysses* was "the number one novel in the twentieth century."

Number one in what way? Number of people who actually read it? Number of people who simply considered it number one? Unknown, at least to me.

There are high school teachers "teaching" *Ulysses*. I'd like to know—how and, most of all, why? Before you look at the opening line of the book you ought to have a knowledge of the geography and history of Dublin and Ireland, you ought to know your way around Catholicism and, maybe, some Judaism (out of respect to Leopold Bloom).

We annually commemorate *Ulysses* because the action, the story, takes place in one day, June 16, 1904. It *is* a story, a very simple story, in its broad outlines. It has a structure that is based generally, very generally, on Homer's *Odyssey*.

But there are layers and themes and connotations that, if you're in the mood, will keep you busy the rest of your life. Because I grew up in Limerick, the only city in Ireland with an anti-Semitic blot on its escutcheon, I've followed the Jewish thread in *Ulysses*. In January 1904 a Limerick priest, John Creagh, stirred the people up against the Jews who, he said, had shed Christian blood. Richard Ellmann says, "Eighty members of the Jewish community were driven out, and only forty were left. Then Creagh was withdrawn from the community."

(That same Creagh, obviously a madman and not the first to be tolerated by the church, was then sent to Australia where he preached against the aborigines.)

If Leopold Bloom is Jewish and anti-Semitism a theme in *Ulysses*, why did Joyce fail to mention the Limerick incident? He must have known about it. Ellmann tells us he did, and that makes it gospel. (If, like me, you want to pursue the Jewish connection, there's a book by Ira B. Nadel, *Joyce and the Jews*, University of Iowa Press, 1989.) Again, the answer is unknown.

Beware the solemnity that might descend on gatherings of Joyceans on June 16. The man himself was anything but solemn and his shade would surely groan if he could witness the extremes of academia in his name. I think he'd enjoy the book you hold in your hand. He'd give Isaiah Sheffer a pat on the back for all those Bloomsdays at Symphony Space where readers and listeners/spectators have sailed on carpets of verbal delight.

I was there at The Creation on June 16, 1982.

Twenty-three years!

May Isaiah forgive me for missing three Bloomsdays in all those years, though I want to remind His Lordship that my brother and I flew from Chicago Just For The Day in 1988.

You don't have to be an actor to read on the Symphony Space stage. I've stood at a microphone with beer salesmen, accountants, The Retired, businessmen, editors, and even, God help us, professors who knew what they were reading and who, offstage, could explicate.

But the professors did not explicate. It wouldn't be tolerated. Yes, yes, there are people (very few) who read assigned passages with no idea of context but they are loved for being there and for their whispered determination that someday they'll read this damn book. It's all right. There are people who read bits of the Bible on Sundays but who among us has read the whole thing?

Look! *Ulysses* is more than a book. It's an event—and that upsets purists, but who's stopping them from retiring to quiet places for an orgy of textual analysis?

I will read at "Bloomsday on Broadway" as long as Isaiah permits me and as long as I can croak out Joyce's wondrous words.

Over the years we've aged, the hair whitening or graying, and many of us have long passed the age at which Joyce died, fifty-eight. Joyce's work has liberated many an artist while his life stands as a lesson for all of us. He suffered greatly: the growing failure of his eyes, the growing madness of his daughter. All his days he skirmished for pennies and fought pitched battles for his art. He was a family man, fiercely tribal, and we must not forget he was driven by love.

Did he love Ireland? As the squirrel loves the nut.

Did he love Catholicism? Imagine his work without it.

Do we love James Joyce?

Watch for the explosion around the world on June 16, 2004, centenary of the Bloom/Dedalus meandering around Dublin and the umpteenth expression of Molly Bloom's triumphant *Yes*.

Introduction

Isaiah Sheffer

There are not many literary holidays that stand out in the calendar year. The twenty-third of April, thought to be William Shakespeare's birthday (as well as the date of his death), is one, and it's a fine spring day for writing a sonnet to your beloved, or walking in the park where birds do sing, hey ding a-ding a-ding. Calendars noting authors' birth dates remind you to honor your favorite writer in whatever way seems appropriate.

But there is only one annual commemoration of a fictional date, a date in which something happened *in a book*. As far as I know, there are no celebrations of the day Huck Finn and Jim set out on a raft in the Mississippi, or the day Ishmael made a fateful decision and signed on board Captain Ahab's *Pequod*, or even the day Saul Bellow's hero Augie March failed to seize the day.

Yet, the sixteenth of June, the day on which James Joyce sets all the action of his epic, *Ulysses*, has, for some reason, turned into a major literary event, "Bloomsday," celebrated each year all over the world, from Dublin to New York and around and down to Sydney, Australia. And we may well ask "what is that reason?", which is also a way of asking just what is so special about *Ulysses* that causes otherwise sane people to want to live inside it for a day each year, whether by reading its pages, listening to actors wrestle with its linguistic challenges, tracing the fictional footsteps of its protagonist through the actual or imagined neighborhoods of 1904 Dublin, or even eating fried kidneys for breakfast?

The biographers tell us that Joyce chose the date of June 16, 1904, for his chronicle of Leopold Bloom, Stephen Dedalus, and Molly Bloom because it was on that date that he first walked out with his own inspiration for Molly, Nora Barnacle, who would be his lifelong companion and mother of his children. But he may also have chosen to set his "chaffering allincluding most farraginous chronicle" on a long day, a spacious day, five days before the summer solstice, when, in the latitude of Dublin, Ireland, the daylight lingers into late evening, and there's room for everything.

Room for everything...? Yes, that may be the first reason for the unique status of *Ulysses* that encourages the lovely madness of celebrating Bloomsday each year. The novel *is* "allincluding." Think of a human feeling, a part of the body, a bodily function, an activity of man- or womankind, and the odds are very good that you'll find at least a reference to it, if not a deep exploration, somewhere in the pages of Joyce's creation. Sports, sex, politics, cooking, parenthood, sons, siblings, daughters, lovers, death and burial, imagination, swimming, streetcar noise, newspaper ads, religion, capital punishment, sado-masochism, butchers, cocoa, Greeks, trees, Jews, Catholics, Protestants, restaurant menus, outhouses, music, books, flirtation, drink, fantasy, cosmetics, bath salts, school, anti-Semitism, xenophobia, song lyrics, violence, fireworks, dogs, cats, rats, cows, protest marches, ferryboat accidents, jealousy, or philology— they're all in there somewhere, and that's only the beginning of what could be a very long list!

A second reason could be that the central characters of *Ulysses* are people we can deeply identify with in one way or another. The first time I read the book I was a young man not too far from Stephen Dedalus's age. Like him, I had recently experienced the death of my mother, and I felt very close to the young schoolteacher, dressed in mourner's black, moping his way through the city's streets or walking along the beach with his ashplant walking-stick, watching the waves ripple and thinking about mortality. At another point in life, when I had become the father of a daughter, I found myself resonating with Mr. Leopold Bloom and his worries about his young filly, silly Milly. And where is the married couple who cannot identify with some aspect of the marriage of Molly and Poldy, its stresses, its contradictions of spunkiness and sterility, its ultimate basic soundness?

A third reason for wanting to dwell in the world of *Ulysses* for at least one day a year is all the rest of the people in it! By which I mean, the enjoyment of encountering the hundreds of minor characters who people its pages and parade through the neighborhoods of Dublin and the hours of Bloom's day. What a collage of portraits, small and large! Some of my favorites: the outrageous and blasphemous mocker Buck Mulligan; young Master Dignam, whose father Paddy was buried this morning, now thoughtfully making his way to the butcher shop; Miss Douce and Miss Kennedy, the twin barmaid sirens; the cyclopean superpatriot citizen; Blazes Boylan, the coarse superstud; Bella Cohen, the whoremistress of Nighttown; Gerty, the twilight temptress of the seaside; the superior, the very reverend Father Conmee, S. J., the pedestrian priest whose long walk provides the backbone to the "Wandering Rocks" episode; poor Mr. Denis Breen, who walks the avenues with a protest sign reading "U.p. up"; Nannetti, the Irish-Italian printer; Professor MacHugh, the rhetorician; or the amply named passer-by Cashel Boyle O'Connor Fitzmaurice Tisdall Farrell—these are only a baker's dozen of the hundreds (thousands?) of vividly limned figures who populate the sixteenth of June, 1904, in Dublin and whom you can figuratively greet like old friends when you partake of a Bloomsday celebration.

If a book as long as *Ulysses* were of a single texture it would probably not engender the same kind of passions and obsessions. But since each of the eighteen sections of Joyce's masterpiece has its own style and form and linguistic distinctiveness, the silent reader or the listener to a Bloomsday reading encounters endless variety, and never grows bored or weary. A lifelong reader whose familiarity with the text is deep can still pick up *Ulysses*, riffle through its pages, and be confronted with a bounteous buffet of literary flavors to choose from: the unpunctuated stream of consciousness of a young man strolling the strand in the "Proteus" section; the howling headlines and tabloid paragraphs of the newspaper episode; the interlocking jigsaw puzzle of "Wandering Rocks"; the over-sweet Victorian lady's magazine prose of "Nausicaa"; the phantasmagoric play script of the Nighttown "Circe" episode, in which the italicized stage directions provide some of the biggest laughs; the cool, exceedingly precise and detailed scientific questions and answers of the homecoming scene in "Ithaca"; the sonic experimentation and fragmented musicality of the "Sirens" episode; the incredible experience of watching the English language itself gestate and evolve from pre-Anglo-Saxon through Chaucerian, Elizabethan, Swiftian, and Dickensian parodies to jazz-age scat in the "Oxen of the Sun" section; and right on up to Molly Bloom's let-it-all-hang-out free association as the book ends. What a choice of treats!

Some people's fun with *Ulysses* may, of course, be based on the puzzle-lover's joy of figuring out complicated structures. Whole library shelves are devoted to books that help the intellectually curious reader to comprehend the architecture of Joyce's ambitious undertaking. Understanding the eighteen-episode structure as a series of six triads, each embodying a progression of thesis, antithesis, and synthesis; or, if you want to see it another way, a triptych with a big central panel and two smaller panels on either side; that is, a three-episode prologue about Stephen Dedalus's morning, twelve central episodes detailing Mr. Bloom's day and containing several near-misses as he and Stephen almost—but don't quite—meet, until at the very end they finally come face to face in the book's climactic moment, and a three-episode epilogue in which the two men are together for a while, separate, and continue to coexist only in Molly's nighttime thoughts.

Joyce himself gave great impetus to this kind of analytic appreciation of his book by allowing a schematic plan of the book to be published, detailing the ways in which each episode has not only its distinctive literary voice, but also its own part of the body, its own color, its own symbols, its own correspondence with the little journey that Bloom's bar of soap makes on its way through his various pants and suit pockets, and its own parallels with figures and events in Homer's *Odyssey*. I must confess that the first time I set out to read through the entire book I armed myself with these guides, side by side with my *Ulysses*. But after a while I came to feel, as most readers probably do, that the training wheels could be removed and I could keep pedaling without their aid.

James Joyce is said to have predicted that people would be puzzling out his *Ulysses* for many years to come, and for me it continues to be the case that with each new reading, and with each year that I direct actors in Symphony Space's June 16 celebration, "Bloomsday on Broadway," I find myself discovering new connections, new reverberations, and new meanings in small details and large themes—as more blanks in the crossword puzzle get filled in. That unnamed man flirting with the flower-shop salesgirl in the "Wandering Rocks" episode is of course Blazes Boylan on his way to his afternoon rehearsal/assignation with Molly Bloom! Several of the somber-suited Dublin men in attendance at the Glasnevin cemetery in the morning "Hades" episode turn out to be on the list (if you can believe that list) of Molly Bloom's amorous conquests, catalogued so fully in the "Ithaca" section's catechisms! Stephen's unorthodox theory of Shakespeare's *Hamlet*, expounded so calculatingly and eloquently to his National Library cronies in the "Scylla and Charybdis" scene, with its focus on the two Hamlets, father and son, King and Prince, has more and more resonances, each time one reads or hears it, with the drama of two Dedaluses, father and son, and even more with the central theme of *Ulysses*, the spiritual father-and-son relationship between Bloom and Stephen.

Compelling human interest, dazzling variety, emotional identification, the rich palimpsest of people, from the book's complex major protagonists to the tiniest vivid word—portraits of background figures in the streets and saloons, the intellectual challenge of mastering the structure and details of a book it took Joyce almost ten years to write—all of these are partial explanations for the reading public's continuing attraction to James Joyce's *Ulysses*. Nevertheless, it remains the case that for many people, including quite a large proportion of English-major college graduates, the book has remained unread, or half-read, for a variety of reasons.

It's a big book, and if you flip randomly through its pages in a library or bookstore, you're playing a tricky game of literary roulette. You may get lucky as your eyeball comes to rest on a page that looks easy enough to comprehend, with narrative description and clear dialogue that take you right into the story and its delights. Or, if you're not as lucky, you may hit upon a page that's far more difficult to penetrate. What is this? Where are we, and what's going on? And this may be discouraging enough to make you assign Joyce's epic to your private list of books that you mean to get around to reading one day—maybe.

What a shame for that to happen to anyone. But there is one surefire, proven, and time-tested way of overcoming one's fear of "that big, forbidding, incomprehensible epic" that you didn't manage to master in college. And that is to hear sections of it, or all of it, read aloud by good actors.

This was the original idea behind the annual literary event that has been taking place at Peter Norton Symphony Space, a performing arts center on Manhattan's Upper West Side, since June 16, 1982. Those who know *Ulysses* well will enjoy hearing chunks of it read by Broadway, television, and film actors who enjoy sinking their teeth once each year into finer and more challenging lines than they usually get to speak. Those who are new to Joyce's work, or awed or frightened or just simply bewildered by it, can be swept up and carried into Bloom's world by the voices, the intelligence, and the brimming enthusiasm of terrific actors.

James Joyce had a lifetime of eye trouble and near-blindness, and scholars and biographers have pointed out that this reality helped make his artistry more aural than visual. His passion was for music, especially vocal music (most especially the tenor repertoire), and he might well have had a singing career himself. His delight was in the sound of words. And for this reason, the words of Joyce, all the different prose styles he mastered, and his poetry as well, come most alive when read aloud.

The big revelation to most people who encounter *Ulysses* in a "Bloomsday on Broadway" reading is that James Joyce is *funny*! Year after year, the mail that pours in from listeners to the public radio broadcasts of "Bloomsday" stresses this reaction. What looked forbidding on the page turns out to be hilarious on the stage or on the radio.

What is it that's so funny? Well, almost everything, but here are a few favorite examples:

- The three different meowings of Mr. Bloom's cat:
    Mkgnao!
    Mrkgnao! and
    Mrkrgnao!;

— Molly Bloom's reply to her husband's definition of "metempsychosis":
  "O rocks, tell us in plain words!";

— Bantam Lyons' misunderstanding of Leopold Bloom's statement that he is going to "throw away" a piece of paper, a chance remark that Lyons misinterprets as a tip to bet on Throwaway, an outside long shot in the Ascot Gold Cup horse race, a bet whose results will cause Bloom violent trouble later in the day;

— The noisy rhetorical competition of the journalists in the newspaper sequence, each trying to outdo the others in savvy sarcasm and verbal swordsmanship;

— The extravagant description of the figure, clothing, and appurtenances of the cyclopean patriot citizen, bedecked with the trappings of all the great Irish heroes from Patrick Shakespeare to The Man Who Broke the Bank at Monte Carlo;

— The pub drinker's exclamation after his first drink of the day, "I was blue mouldy for the want of that pint. Declare to God I could hear it hit the pit of my stomach with a click";

— The cascading deluge of words that follows the three-word question, "Did it flow?" as Joyce explains the consequences of Bloom turning on the tap to get the water for his and Stephen's late-night cocoa, by describing the workings of the entire Dublin water system from the farthest reaches of the watershed through all the streams, aqueducts, pipes, hydrants, risers, and pumping stations of the Hibernian metropolis.

To look out from the stage at Symphony Space at a theatre full of hundreds of listeners, several dozen holding printed copies of the text and following along with the readers, is to take in a sea of attentive and frequently smiling faces, smiling at the pleasure of a particular passage, or just smiling with a look of wild cognition that says clearly, "Oh! Now I get it!"

When we first began presenting "Bloomsday on Broadway" we made some basic artistic decisions that have remained in force for more than two decades. We did not want this to be one of those happenings at which enthusiasts take turns reading a page or two of a classic and then step down to give the next reader his or her turn, regardless of the content or meaning of what is being read. No, this would be carefully chosen excerpts from *Ulysses*, thoughtfully cast, crafted and shaped, directed and rehearsed, read by an annual assemblage of some of the best actors in New York, supplemented here and there by avid Joyceans who, if not professional actors, would contribute enthusiasm and authenticity.

We wanted Bloomsday to be a lengthy event, commensurate with the long novel it celebrates. But exactly *how* long should it be? Despite some press accounts describing our June 16 tradition, we have never read through the entire book from start to finish in any one year. Even though Symphony Space likes presenting the occasional marathon musical or literary event—such as the twelve-hour "Wall-to-Wall" concert series, another of our flagship events, with a tradition that's even longer than the twenty-three years of "Bloomsdays"—reading all of *Ulysses* would take something like thirty-two hours—a little too much for even the hearty and adventurous Symphony Space production staff.

The longest "Bloomsday" was around sixteen or seventeen hours in duration, beginning at eight o'clock in the morning and going on until after two the next morning, but most have been much shorter. None has been less than five hours long. When the sixteenth of June falls on a weeknight when most people have to get up for work the next day, a typical "Bloomsday on Broadway" reading at Symphony Space begins at five or six in the evening and goes until midnight (or a little after, since Molly Bloom's nighttime thoughts, which end the book, are said to be beyond time, in the numberless wee hours).

But a Saturday or Sunday "Bloomsday," when audiences and our radio station broadcast partners are available for a longer day's journey into Nighttown and beyond, offers a more spacious opportunity to do a ten- or twelve-hour literary extravaganza, covering more of the text and employing the talents of seventy or eighty readers. For the 2004 centennial of that great fictional day, June 16, 1904, which happens to fall on a Wednesday, we will go from noon to midnight (or a little after) with one hundred actors.

Since our way of celebrating Bloomsday is to create a literary event in a New York City theatre, we cannot, as they do in Dublin, conduct a citywide trek from place to place mentioned in the book, dressed in the clothing of 1904, nor do we get people together in a restaurant on the morning of June 16 to duplicate Leopold Bloom's breakfast of "the inner organs of beasts and fowls." We do, however, have our theatre's café offer the wine and cheese that Bloom enjoys for lunch as well as a large supply of the good Irish ale that lubricates the book and our actors and audience. The historic McSorley's saloon in downtown Manhattan has a lovely tradition of donating a few cases to Symphony Space for the enjoyment of the Joycean revelers.

Though we do not costume our readers, they are free to dress as they see fit, and in 2003 an actor who had been assigned the role of Bloom got himself up in a dark suit and bowler hat. On his way uptown to do his reading he was recognized and greeted by many New York City subway riders who cried out across the platform, "Hello there, Mr. Bloom!"

Choosing the material to be read at "Bloomsday" presents an annual creative challenge. On many occasions, we have devoted a few hours, at least, to "A Whirlwind Tour of All Eighteen Episodes of *Ulysses*," choosing excerpts from each, and introducing each segment with just enough background on the time of day, the literary style, and the episode's place in the intertwining days of Stephen, Bloom, and Molly to give the theatre audience and the public radio listeners some helpful orientation. The Whirlwind Tour is very useful for people who are new to the book, giving them an overview and enticing them to return on their own to episodes that catch their fancy.

But most years we also seek to go a little deeper into a particular section and read one or two episodes in their entirety, even if that means allocating a sizable chunk of our running time. The morning episodes are the shortest, and episodes get longer as the book goes on. Stephen's early-morning seaside walk, the "Proteus" episode, is a manageable half-hour read, start to finish. The complete "Cyclops" barroom episode, from the early evening, takes a very full three-hour stretch to encompass the violent confrontation between Bloom and the citizen as well as all the parodies and riffs that spin off from the talk in the pub. Similarly, the interlocking urban snapshots of the midday "Wandering Rocks" section require about three hours to perambulate.

And some "Bloomsdays" have an overriding theme that determines the *Ulysses* selections. For example, when June 16 happens to fall on a Father's Day, we might focus on passages related to the theme of paternity, in all its many aspects, a theme that was quite important to James Joyce. At two very special "Bloomsdays," I was joined as cohost by the eminent translator of Homer's *Odyssey*, Robert Fagles, and the script for the day was devoted to demonstrating the specific parallels between the adventures of Homer's Odysseus and Joyce's Mr. Bloom.

To keep "Bloomsday on Broadway" fresh each year we also frequently go outside the text of the novel and read a bit from other works of Joyce. A section from *A Portrait of the Artist as a Young Man* lets us meet the younger Stephen Dedalus; spoken or sung settings from Joyce's *Chamber Music* poetry volume offer another kind of insight into the mind and art of young Joyce/Dedalus. And to show the world where some of the experimental linguistic inventions of *Ulysses*, Bloom's *day* book, were leading, we have often included at least a sampling of Joyce's next book, the dream-language *night* book, *Finnegans Wake*.

A little-known fact in the history of Symphony Space is that our most famous artistic program, *Selected Shorts: A Celebration of the Short Story*, which features actors reading classic and contemporary short fiction and which National Public Radio broadcasts across America, was a result of "Bloomsday." One fateful year we had an actress read a short story from Joyce's *Dubliners*, and a new program was born.

Over the years, many special segments have been created for "Bloomsday on Broadway": settings of Joyce texts by twentieth- and twenty-first-century composers; a session on food and cooking in Joyce's works; an inquiry by Ira Nadel, the author of *Joyce and the Jews*, into the question of how the greatest Jewish character in literature came to be created by an Irishman; a revealing portrait of the real-life prototype for stately, plump Buck Mulligan—the colorful Oliver St. John Gogarty; and an investigation of the real relationship between James Joyce and William Butler Yeats.

One year it occurred to me that our annual celebration of life, love, and language could also encompass an entirely non-Joycean two- or three-hour segment, under the patronage of St. James Aloysius Joyce, surveying Irish poetry from the earliest songs of Ossian to the work of such contemporary bards as Seamus Heaney and Paul Muldoon. Many fine actors read hours of wonderful poetry, but we ran into some resistance from a few Bloomsday regulars who reproved us in the press and in letters, saying that we had better not forget that Bloomsday is about *Ulysses*! It seems we've become part of a tradition, and people have their recurring needs.

Another basic artistic decision about our Bloomsday event has often caused considerable stress during casting and in rehearsals. I'm referring to the direction that I have always given the actors: "No Irish accents!" Recruiting a top Broadway actor to be part of our June 16 readings, I am frequently met by the reply, "Gee, I'm sorry, I'd love to be there, but I can't do a good Irish accent." And then I must carefully explain our policy: this is "Bloomsday *on Broadway*." We're Americans; some of us are Irish-Americans, others are Jewish-Americans, African-Americans, Latinos, immigrants from everywhere—and each of us should sound like what we are. Yes, we do have quite a few actors here today who are from Dublin or Galway or Belfast or Limerick, but each actor should glory in his own sound and not try to "do the Irish."

This notion has been resisted, to my consternation, by some American actors who insist (rightly, in some instances) that they can do a perfect Irish accent, and why shouldn't they, when at the next microphone stands Fionnula Flanagan or one of the McCourt brothers? It's a challenge to persuade them that we *want* the mixture of sounds, that it gives our celebration its distinctive New

York Broadway flavor. It's more than sufficient to let the rhythms of Joyce's language speak for themselves, without any overlay. As for the otherwise fine actors whose "Irish accents" make them sound like leprechauns in a bad St. Patrick's Day beer commercial, the less said the better. But the policy stands.

Thousands of people who have never set foot in Symphony Space at a "Bloomsday" event have instead enjoyed it through its radio broadcast. It's a very different kind of experience, according to people who have done both. At Symphony Space you can witness the day-long procession of actors being ushered to their onstage seats, where they await their turn at one of the reading stands and microphones that spread across the stage. You can watch the interplay between the actors, all within the framework of the stage décor: huge lithograph blow-ups of "The James Joyce Playing Cards" created by the Joyce biographer Richard Ellmann and the graphic designer Rosita Fanto, in which Molly Bloom, naturally, is the Queen of Hearts and James Joyce is the Joker. You can visit our café, transformed for the day into Barney Kiernan's tavern, and there see pairs of readers for the next segment rehearsing their cues, while readers from the previous segment enjoy a well-earned pint.

Radio listeners tell us that listening to the *Ulysses* broadcast is a much more private experience. Whether at home and following along in the text, or driving in your car toward whatever other plans you have for June 16, it is the words alone that reach you, and it is your own imagination that conjures up the Dublin scenes.

The social scene in the offstage café area at Symphony Space can sometimes get a little raucous as the day and the evening roll on. Despite the efficient stage managers greeting the actors, signing them in, and directing them toward their partners, their rehearsals, and eventually onto the stage, and despite the loudspeakers carrying the readings from the stage, and despite the large signs that read "SHHH—SERIOUS LITERARY EVENT IN PROGRESS," a party atmosphere often prevails. For a certain segment of the New York theatre community, backstage at "Bloomsday" is your chance to see some old friends once a year.

Whatever the content or format of any particular Bloomsday, whether or not it begins, as the book does, with "Stately, plump Buck Mulligan," it most definitely has to end with the words of Molly Bloom. As Joyce is supposed to have said, "Molly gets the last word." At the shorter Bloomsdays, we've had at least the final hour of the "Penelope" episode, Molly's wakeful, erotic, insomniac nighttime thoughts as her husband, the traveler Leopold, sleeps curled up beside her, his head at her feet.

When time has permitted, at the longer events, we have invited wonderful actresses, including Anne Meara, Terry Donnelly, and, most often, Fionnula Flanagan, to attempt the prodigious feat of reading the uninterrupted, uncensored, and almost unpunctuated forty-five-page monologue that ends Bloomsday. The Molly monologue usually begins after ten p.m. or even eleven, and it will go on until almost two in the morning.

Before Molly begins, I am charged with issuing the annual "public radio language advisory" to warn radio listeners that what they are about to hear contains sexually, anatomically, and scatalogically explicit words that may require parental guidance. I tell the story of the *Ulysses* court case and remind listeners that in 1933 a United States federal district court judge ruled that *Ulysses* is not obscene. But I tell parents who fear the possible deleterious effects of having their impressionable children listen in on Molly's thinking to send the kids out in the city streets to play.

An annual ritual has developed around this closing. Many audience members who have been in their seats throughout the marathon event leap up and head for home as the previous episode is ending so they can experience the Molly Bloom episode as Molly and Leopold Bloom do—at home, in bed, safe, returned from an adventurous literary and theatrical odyssey. But a sturdy band of adventurers remain in their seats and stick it out to the last words of the epic.

It is a rare and wondrous experience to be in the theatre at one in the morning, after a long day of literature, love, life, and language, and to feel the attention the audience invariably radiates toward the solitary female figure onstage. As Molly Bloom, that actress expresses vividly the depth, the humanity, the affirmation at the heart of Joyce's compassionate, funny, lovely work. I'm usually exhausted by that point, but if I chance to think, "Whew! Hey...are we going to do this all over again next year?", my answer will probably be, as it has been for more than two decades, "yes I will Yes."

Sylvia Beach and Joyce outside Shakespeare and Company, on the rue de l'Odéon, Paris, circa 1920.

First Reactions

1

Few periods in the history of art and science have witnessed change more tumultuous than that known as modernism at the beginning of the twentieth century. As Joyce was writing *Ulysses*, Einstein was bending light rays, Freud was articulating a new language of the unconscious mind, Schoenberg was creating atonal harmonic sequences, and the Cubists were fracturing the two-dimensional picture plane with geometric abstraction. The first reactions to each of these occurrences were, at best, conflicted. *Manet and the Post-Impressionists*, the first major British exhibition of the work of Cézanne, Gauguin, and van Gogh, organized by Bloomsbury artist and critic Roger Fry in 1910, was openly reviled. Picasso's *Les Demoiselles d'Avignon* (1907) shocked a skittish public in 1916 at the Salon d'Antin, monumentally breaching the laws of classical composition and perspective. On the literary front, the publication of *Ulysses* caused such uproar that the book was banned in the United Kingdom and the United States.

Because change is seldom sudden and historical periods are often indeterminate, ascribing dates to these periods can be arbitrary. There are exceptions. On February 2, 1922, the date that *Ulysses* was first published in its entirety, the course of English literature changed forever. A select few saw the genius in it. The critic Edmund Wilson said of *Ulysses* (*The New Republic*, 1922) that, in addition to diverging from traditional literary forms, and, most importantly, raising the standard of the novel, "It is, in short, perhaps the most faithful X-ray ever taken of the ordinary human consciousness."

Ulysses was first published in France, in English. On the morning of Joyce's fortieth birthday, his Paris publisher, Sylvia Beach, hand-delivered to him a single copy of the first edition of *Ulysses*. But it was twelve years before a reader in the English-speaking world could legally obtain a copy. During those years Joyce waged an ardent campaign for the survival of his novel and for freedom of speech. The case against *Ulysses* was symptomatic of the Western world's difficulty adjusting to the promises and perils of contemporary life, and emblematic of the struggle to unyoke the harness of the past. Virginia Woolf's assertion that "on or about December, 1910, human character changed," a reference to Fry's exhibition, acknowledges the confluence of circumstances in which Joyce battled for more than a decade against a three-pronged enemy: obscenity laws, copyright laws, and the discretionary powers of customs and postal officials. In 1933, United States District Court Judge John Woolsey ruled that *Ulysses* was not obscene, paving the way for legal publication in the United States.

That the world in general had changed forever in the early twentieth century is indisputable. By the end of World War I, progress in the Victorian sense, an immutable force built on the concept of free will and personal responsibility, was dead. The relentless destruction perpetrated by civilized nations upon one another during the war obliterated the familiar sense of order and morality that had long prevailed. When the war was over, Winston Churchill wrote, "Torture and Cannibalism were the only two expedients that the civilized, scientific, Christian States had been able to deny themselves: and they were of doubtful utility." Lenin and the Bolsheviks seized control of Russia in October 1917, achieving a Communist revolution that would promote Marxist government throughout Europe, in many cases by force.

Joyce recognized continental Europe as a center of early modernism and by 1904 he had left Ireland for good. His disassociation from insular Dublin life and Irish politics gave Joyce entry to an international literary circle. However, throughout his life he maintained a complicated relationship to his native land, embracing and rejecting the influences that had shaped his art. In *Ulysses*, Stephen refers to the cracked looking glass of a servant as a symbol for Irish art. In Ireland, Joyce considered himself an outsider, and although he returned many times, he refused to acknowledge political ties. He was fascinated by the country's history but exhibited disdain for the parochialism of his countrymen. Joyce said, "When the soul of a man is born in this country there are nets flung at it to hold it back from flight. You talk to me of nationality, language, religion. I shall try to fly by those nets." Joyce started writing *Ulysses* in 1915, the year he moved to Zurich, having lived in Trieste for most of the preceding decade. It was his intention to write a "European" work of fiction, yet in the realms of religion and music, Joyce retained his Irishness. Although he rejected Catholicism, his Catholic education was something to which he attributed importance. His earlier career in singing and his poetry are characterized by the Irish traits of tenderness and melancholy, traces of which remained in his later work. The writer Djuna Barnes remarked that she could hear the singer in *Ulysses*, and Edmund Wilson described Joyce's style as "symphonic rather than narrative."

Early on, Joyce's writing attracted the attention of Ezra Pound, who introduced Joyce to Margaret Anderson and Jane Heap, the editors of the American magazine *The Little Review*. They published parts of *Ulysses* in the U.S. starting in 1918. By 1920 this venture had cost them dearly—they were tried for the publication of obscenity and reprimanded by the Society for the Suppression of Vice. In 1922, Sylvia Beach, an American expatriate living in Paris and the proprietor of the Shakespeare and Company bookshop, offered to publish *Ulysses*. One thousand copies were printed and immediately dispatched to international destinations. Later that year, the Egoist Press in London undertook a second printing of 2,000 copies, which were printed in France. New York postal officials seized and burned 500 copies. In 1923, the Egoist Press commissioned a third printing of 500 copies, 499 of which were seized by English Customs Authorities. *Ulysses* was bootlegged; pirated copies, rife with errors and omissions, were sold underground. One such disreputable publisher, Samuel Roth, became the object of Joyce's wrath when he openly sold the contraband. A protest against the pirated version of *Ulysses* was signed by hundreds of the world's leading writers.

The degree to which reviewers missed Joyce's meaning is in direct proportion to the degree of fame *Ulysses* immediately attracted. The first and least interesting misconception was that Joyce had written a book of pornography. Beyond this, an inability to discern a purpose to the structure of *Ulysses* unnerved many readers. This omission was intentional on Joyce's part and although the underlying structures of *Ulysses* are extremely complex—possibly overly systemized, as Joyce himself commented—he kept his scheme secret.

Peggy Guggenheim's order for a first edition copy of Ulysses *from Shakespeare and Company, 1922.*

He boasted that the unraveling of the themes and structures would occupy scholars and professors for years to come and thus ensure the author's immortality. In 1930, Joyce allowed Stuart Gilbert to publish part of *Ulysses'* structure and later claimed that his decision, made as a publicity ploy, had been a terrible mistake. Parallels between the *Odyssey* and *Ulysses* were eventually recognized as tributes to Homer and are still widely discussed today.

Ulysses contains instances of words or passages depicting sex organs, bodily functions, and other human traits that were deemed objectionable. Joyce's scathingly frank assessment of daily life in all its banality rankled the public. Virginia Woolf wrote, "Mr. Joyce's indecency in *Ulysses* seems to me the conscious and calculated indecency of a desperate man who feels that in order to breathe he must break the windows. At moments, when the window is broken, he is magnificent. But what a waste of energy!" T. S. Eliot exalted Joyce when he said that *Ulysses* had "destroyed the whole of the nineteenth century."

"Bloom's day is uncensored, very well," Ezra Pound remarked, but he had little patience for the prudishness of *Ulysses'* opponents. He argued that Joyce had presented the nature of a particular time and place with such lucidity that "the imaginary Chinaman or denizen of the forty-first century could without works of reference gain a very good idea of the scene and habits portrayed," and that for the sake of a few words the world could not afford to deny or dilute Joyce's genius. In 1933–1934, Random House successfully defended Joyce's novel against obscenity charges and published *Ulysses* in the Modern Library. Judge John M. Woolsey wrote eloquently of Joyce's novel, and of his genius, in the famous decision that lifted the ban on *Ulysses* in the U.S. In his foreword to the 1934 edition, the counsel for Random House, Morris L. Ernst, wrote the following:

It would be difficult to overestimate the importance of Judge Woolsey's decision. For decades the censors have fought to emasculate literature. They have tried to set up the sensibilities of the prudery-ridden as a criterion for society, have sought to reduce the reading matter of adults to the level of adolescents and subnormal persons, and have nurtured evasions and sanctimonies.

Pound, in his essay entitled "*Ulysses*," asserts, "The best criticism of any work, to my mind the only criticism of any work of art that is of any permanent or even moderately durable value, comes from the creative writer or artist who does the next job.... Joyce and perhaps Henry James are critics of Flaubert." Joyce had read Flaubert and he greatly admired the poet Dante. He had studied Dano-Norwegian to read Ibsen and his first published critical writing is an essay on the Ibsen play, *When We Dead Awaken*. Upon meeting the poet William Butler Yeats, Joyce expressed his regret that Yeats was "too old to be influenced by him." Yeats later returned the compliment by admitting that he hadn't been able to finish *Ulysses*.

Joyce felt that his true contemporary audience was the other writers and artists of his day and remained steadfast in his campaign to have his work read. He wrote letters, collected the reviews, and monitored every detail of the *Ulysses* saga. The more heated the response, the more it pleased him. He sent copies to friends and acquaintances. His friend Robert McAlmon wrote a review without bothering to finish the book, and informed Joyce he was planning to throw *Ulysses* out the window. Joyce wrote back, "Don't throw *Ulysses* out of the window as you threaten. Pyrrhus was killed in Argos like that. Also Socrates might be passing in the street." In honor of the Bloomsday centenary, June 16, 2004, it seems a fitting gesture to glance back to the bank and shoals upon which the barriers of traditional representational form in fiction were dashed and James Joyce laid his self-conscious claim to immortality. The response to *Ulysses* was immediate and extreme. Writer and literary critic Malcolm Cowley described it using the metaphor of a stone dropped into water: there was a moment of silence, the stone was dropped, "then all the frogs who inhabited the pool began to talk at once."

Brancusi's drawings of Joyce, one of which appeared in Tales Told of Shem and Sham, *1929.*

It is an entirely new thing—neither what the eye sees nor the ear hears, but what the rambling mind thinks and imagines from moment to moment. He has certainly surpassed in intensity any novelist of our time. —*W. B. Yeats*

In a single chapter he discharges all the clichés of the English language like an uninterrupted river. —*Ezra Pound*

Never did I read such tosh. As for the first 2 chapters we will let them pass, but the 3rd 4th 5th 6th—merely the scratching of pimples on the body of the bootboy at Claridges. —*Virginia Woolf*

Yet for all its appalling longueurs, "Ulysses" is a work of high genius. Its importance seems to me to lie, not so much in its opening new doors to knowledge—unless in setting an example to Anglo-Saxon writers of putting down everything without compunction—or in inventing new literary forms—Joyce's formula is really, as I have indicated, nearly seventy-five years old—as in its once more setting the standard of the novel so high that it need not be ashamed to take its place beside poetry and drama. "Ulysses" has the effect at once of making everything else look brassy.
—*Edmund Wilson*

It is simply the foulest book that has ever found its way into print.... But what concerns us all...is the appalling fact that our Metropolitan criticism should have been treating such works as those of Mr. Joyce seriously as works of genius. —*Alfred Noyes, reviewing* Ulysses *in the* Manchester Sunday Chronicle

It's a turgid welter of pornography (the rudest schoolboy kind) & unformed & unimportant drivel; & until the raw ingredients of a pudding *make* a pudding, I shall never believe that the raw material of sensation & thought can make a work of art without the cook's intervening. —*Edith Wharton*

———

I say deliberately that it is the most infamously obscene book in ancient or modern literature. The obscenity of Rabelais is innocent compared with its leprous and scabrous horrors. All the secret sewers of vice are canalised in its flood of unimaginable thoughts, images and pornographic words. And its unclean lunacies are larded with appalling and revolting blasphemies directed against the Christian religion and against the name of Christ....The book is already the bible of beings who are exiles and outcasts in this and every civilised country. It is also adopted by the Freudians as the supreme glory of their dirty and degraded cult. —*James Douglas, reviewing* Ulysses *in the Dublin* Sunday Express

———

The trouble is that there are many people who are incapable of distinguishing between the lewd lucubrations and *Ulysses*. I dare say many of them bought *Ulysses* for the sake of passages which, they had been told, were improper. How disappointed they must have been! For the passages they sought are so rare, and are so interwoven in the texture of the book, and are so meaningless by themselves, that the nasty-minded purchasers would find *Ulysses* dull reading, and think themselves swindled. —*Sisley Huddleston*

———

I feel like shouting EUREKA!...Easily the epic of the age.
—*Hart Crane*

It is a stupendous attempt to present us with a truer picture of the human mind than has ever been achieved before, by creating the discontinuous stream of thoughts, habits of mind rising from the past, disturbances caused by the environment, and even suggested by purely physical movements of the body, which pass through the fragmentary and interrupted consciousness of people at every moment. —*Stephen Spender*

GENIUS AND SOCIAL RANK
Virginia Woolf

I rather agree that Joyce is underrated: but never did any book so bore me.
—*Virginia Woolf, referring to* Ulysses, *in a letter dated December 1, 1923*

Virginia Woolf and James Joyce had many things in common. In addition to their contributions to modernist fiction, both bore the distinction of having been called geniuses during their lifetimes, and both paid dearly for their art. Neither was a stranger to madness. They even shared the same birth and death years. As for their differences, two areas stand out: social class and the attention each paid to the other. Woolf was born into privilege and assumed the role of artist among a select circle of the Victorian upper-middle class. For Joyce, circumstances proved more difficult; he lived as an exile on meager means. As for the matter of attentions paid, it is not evident that Joyce commented on Virginia Woolf's writing. The reverse cannot be said.

As installments of Ulysses *appeared in* The Little Review, *Harriet Shaw Weaver approached Leonard and Virginia Woolf asking them to publish Joyce's novel through the Woolfs' Hogarth Press. Woolf's account (Letter to Lytton Strachey, April 23, 1918):*

We've been asked to print Mr Joyce's new novel, every printer in London and most in the provinces having refused. First there's a dog that p's—then there's a man that forths, and one can be monotonous even on that subject—moreover, I don't believe that his method, which is highly developed, means much more than cutting out the explanations and putting in the thoughts between dashes. So I don't think we shall do it.

A few years later, Woolf expressed a different sentiment, although her criticism is hardly veiled (diary, September 20, 1920):

Joyce gives Internals. His novel Ulysses, presents the life of a man in 16 incidents, all taking place (I think) in one day. This, so far as he has seen it is extremely brilliant he says. Perhaps we shall try to publish it. Ulysses, according to Joyce, is the greatest character in history[.] Joyce himself is an insignificant man, wearing very thick eyeglasses, a little like Shaw to look at, dull, self-centered, & perfectly self assured.

On August 26, 1922:

I dislike Ulysses more & more—that is think it more & more unimportant; & don't even trouble conscientiously to make out its meanings. Thank God, I need not write about it.

Woolf was known for having a corrosive tongue. She delivered a more acerbic decree on Ulysses *in the diaries, September 6, 1922:*

I finished Ulysses, & think it a mis-fire. Genius it has I think; but of the inferior water. The book is diffuse. It is brackish. It is pretentious. It is underbred, not only in the obvious sense, but in the literary sense. A first rate writer, I mean, respects writing too much to be tricky; startling; doing stunts. I'm reminded all the time of some callow board school boy, say like Henry Lamb, full of wits & powers, but so self-conscious & egotistical that he loses his head, becomes extravagant, mannered, uproarious, ill at ease, makes kindly people feel sorry for him, & stern ones merely annoyed; & one hopes he'll grow out of it; but as Joyce is 40 this scarcely seems likely.

In his recollection of Woolf, writer Christopher Isherwood raised the question: "Was she the bewitched princess, or the wicked little girl at the tea party—or both, or neither?"

Either way, Woolf clearly acknowledged Joyce's place in letters, if only by the intensity of her dismissals. In her criticism, she assumed a safe bet—using the one incontrovertible fact, that in social status she outranked him, a fact that remains incontestable. For Woolf, Ulysses *could be dismissed as, among other things, the product of a self-educated working-class man.*

Joyce was soon deriving a steady income from *Ulysses* in spite of the fact that it was denied its normal outlets in the English-speaking countries. And, of course, its reputation as a banned book helped the sales. It was saddening, however, to see such a work listed in catalogues of erotica alongside *Fanny Hill*, *The Perfumed Garden* and that everlasting Casanova, not to speak of plain pornography like *Raped on the Rail*. An Irish priest, purchasing *Ulysses*, asked me, "Any other spicy books?" —*Sylvia Beach*

Joyce is remarkable, rather, for equanimity: in spite of the nervous intensity of "Ulysses," there is a real serenity and detachment behind it—we are in the presence of a mind which has much in common with that of a certain type of philosopher, who in his effort to understand the causes of things, to interrelate the different elements of the universe, has reached a point where the ordinary values of good and bad, beautiful and ugly, have been lost in the excellence and beauty of transcendent understanding itself.
—*Edmund Wilson*

Joyce is too near me for me to want to do less than he did in *Ulysses*, in looseness of spirit, and honesty of heart—at least.
—*William Carlos Williams*

I also don't know whether you will enjoy what I have written about *Ulysses*, because I couldn't help telling the world how much I was bored, how I grumbled, how I cursed and how I admired. The 40 pages of non-stop run in the end is a string of veritable psychological peaches. I suppose the devil's grandmother knows so much about the real psychology of a woman. I didn't. —*C. G. Jung*

Ulysses...is a dogged attempt to cover the universe with mud. It is an inverted Victorianism, an attempt to make crossness and dirt succeed where sweetness and light failed, a simplification of the human character in the interests of Hell. —*E. M. Forster (Forster also called* Ulysses *"perhaps the most interesting literary experiment of our day."*)

[*Ulysses*] will immortalize its author with the same certainty that Gargantua and Pantagruel immortalized Rabelais, and *The Brothers Karamazov* Dostoyevsky.... [It] comes nearer to being the perfect revelation of a personality than any book in existence. —*Dr. Joseph Collins, reviewing* Ulysses *in* The New York Times

The sharp beauty and sensitivity of the thing! The matchless details!... His book is steeped in the Elizabethans, his early love, and Latin Church, and some Greek.... It is my opinion that some fanatic will kill Joyce sometime soon for the wonderful things said in *Ulysses*. —*Hart Crane*

Joyce and Sylvia Beach in Shakespeare and Company bookshop, Paris, early 1920s.

"THE NEW CRITICAL MIND"

An article in the April 1922 issue of Vanity Fair *entitled "The New Order of Critical Values" announced that in America, a great Transvaluation of Values had occurred and a new critical mind was in force. This evolution was depicted as an offensive, as a "gang of pirates taking over"—the "tranquil stream of native talent" disturbed by foreign bodies. The article consisted mainly of a chart—excerpted here—in which 201 subjects, chosen to encompass the "whole field of life and thought," were ranked by ten critics selected to represent the new order. Perceived as "...a sort of logarithm table by which the views of these celebrated authorities may be ascertained on almost any subject," the chart was intended to signify the new critical values derived from the ten opinions and, thus, to illustrate the "new critical mind." The evaluations were based on a numerical system, 25 being highest, –25 being lowest, and 0 reflecting ambivalence or possible irrelevance in the mind of the critic. Shakespeare, Bach, and Goethe scored highest; Theodore Roosevelt scored lowest. Dr. Johnson and Krazy Kat were tied, as were Cézanne and Homer. James Joyce weighed in behind Titian and Sophocles (tied), and in front of St. Francis. The article included the brief profiles of the ten "authorities." They are characterized as follows:*

Heywood Broun [columnist, book and theatre critic for the New York *World*], "discourses wittily and humanly on books and plays"; **Henry McBride** [art critic for *The Sun*, *The Dial*], "most hospitable to the modernist"; **H. L. Mencken** [coeditor of *The Smart Set* (1914–23), a guide for the young American intellectual], "most vigorous opponent of the Puritan tradition in American letters"; **George Jean Nathan** [editor; drama critic; left the *New York Herald* to join H. L. Mencken in editing *The Smart Set*], "arch-enemy of all that is sentimental, provincial and pretentious in American drama"; **Burton Rascoe**, "an enthusiastic supporter of modern aesthetic creeds in literature and art"; **Paul Rosenfeld** [music, art, and literary critic], "combines a wide knowledge of the past, with a fervid appreciation of the modern movements in music, letters and painting"; **Gilbert Seldes** [managing editor, *The Dial*], "subjects modern literary experiment to an uncompromising comparison with the accomplishments of the great"; **Deems Taylor** [music critic, *The World*], "is generous enough to the new which seems to him authentic, without losing his actual allegiance to the old"; **Edmund Wilson, Jr.** [contributor, *New Republic* and *Vanity Fair*], "upholds the classic tradition of symmetry and form"; and **Willard Huntington Wright** [author; editor (1912–14) of *The Smart Set*], "in full sympathy with the moderns."

	HB	HMcB	HLM	GJN	BR	PR	GS	DT	EW	WHW	Average
Aeschylus	0	20	20	12	25	24	12	21	20	0	15.4
Aristotle	0	−5	25	15	20	25	21	20	25	21	16.7
Beethoven	0	25	25	25	24	19	0	22	25	25	19.0
Cézanne	0	25	5	2	25	25	17	18	15	25	15.7
Conrad, Joseph	17	5	20	20	20	−8	20	25	10	25	14.4
Dante	0	25	−20	13	25	25	17	12	25	−15	10.7
Dempsey, Jack	8	25	5	10	25	3	1	4	−20	0	6.1
Dickens, Charles	13	25	10	4	5	11	20	18	15	−24	9.7
Eliot, T. S.	0	0	0	0	25	4	17	11	7	0	6.4
Erasmus	0	25	0	0	0	15	1	21	15	0	7.7
Fairbanks, Douglas	6	25	5	0	0	−9	−20	8	−5	−10	0
Flaubert	9	15	20	20	25	17	20	10	15	17	16.8
Franklin, Benjamin	6	20	12	0	10	−11	−22	10	10	2	3.7
Freud, Sigmund	19	4	10	5	2	17	15	12	15	−25	7.4
Gilbert & Sullivan	14	25	22	24	5	4	12	20	15	15	15.6
Gish, Lillian	2	8	17	17	1	−1	−22	5	0	−24	.3
Homer	0	20	20	16	25	25	14	13	20	4	15.7
Ibsen	15	20	10	18	0	19	2	21	17	5	12.7
James, Henry	4	9	10	5	21	10	25	20	15	14	13.3
James, William	8	11	15	4	10	9	1	17	10	−15	7.0
Jefferson, Thomas	17	0	10	12	−15	4	5	10	10	12	6.5
Joan of Arc	15	0	0	−24	0	12	5	23	2	0	3.3
Joyce, James	0	10	15	2	25	13	20	12	13	5	11.5
Krazy Kat	2	0	0	−25	25	0	23	24	2	25	7.6
Lenin	13	15	−25	−25	0	8	8	18	13	−25	0
Matisse	0	18	0	2	20	14	8	6	8	15	9.1
New York Tribune	4	−25	−25	0	0	−25	−5	−14	−25	0	11.5
Nietzsche	5	25	25	13	25	21	25	20	10	21	19.0
Pater, Walter	0	16	5	19	10	10	19	0	5	−10	7.4
Pickford, Mary	5	8	0	0	1	−1	−17	8	0	−18	-1.4
Plato	7	25	25	5	18	25	3	25	25	7	16.5
Raphael	0	25	0	15	0	18	−4	20	12	8	9.4
Roosevelt, T.	7	7	20	20	0	−10	−9	0	−25	−25	-9.5
Ruskin	4	10	−10	7	−25	6	−16	−8	−4	−25	-6.1
Shakespeare	19	25	25	25	25	25	20	22	21	17	22.4
Shaw, G. B.	23	3	15	14	−21	4	23	22	16	−20	7.9
Sophocles	0	25	0	8	18	20	−16	22	23	16	11.6
Stravinsky	14	11	1	2	20	9	6	19	10	−10	8.2
Tagore	−2	0	−20	−20	−25	2	−5	9	1	−25	-8.5
Virgil	0	10	−10	8	6	12	5	5	20	4	6.0
Voltaire	13	25	25	8	3	20	21	21	20	8	16.4
Wells, H. G.	19	0	20	10	0	3	2	23	10	−17	7.8
Wilde, Oscar	11	15	5	16	5	4	16	20	3	10	10.5
Wordsworth	2	20	5	2	−25	8	0	−1	18	−10	1.9
Yeats, W. B.	2	−10	10	2	15	4	22	17	25	3	9.0

"JAMES JOYCE" BY DJUNA BARNES
Vanity Fair, April 1922

Ms. Barnes recounts a meeting with Joyce in the café of the Deux Magots in Paris:

Because he had heard of the suppression of *The Little Review* on account of *Ulysses* and of the subsequent trial, he sat down opposite me, who was familiar with the whole story, ordering a white wine. He began to talk at once. "The pity is," he said, seeming to choose his words for their age rather than their aptness, "the public will demand and find a moral in my book—or worse they may take it in some more serious way, and on the honour of a gentleman, there is not one single serious line in it."

For a moment there was silence. His hands, peculiarly limp in the introductory shake and peculiarly pulpy, running into a thickness that the base gave no hint of, lay, one on the stem of the glass, the other, forgotten, palm out, on the most delightful waistcoat it has ever been my happiness to see. Purple with alternate doe and dog heads. The does, tiny scarlet tongues hanging out over blond lower lips, downed in a light wool, and the dogs no more ferocious or on the scent than any good animal who adheres to his master through the seven cycles of change.

He saw my admiration and he smiled. "Made by the hand of my grandmother for the first hunt of the season" and there was another silence in which he arranged and lit a cigar.

"All great talkers," he said softly, "have spoken in the language of Sterne, Swift or the Restoration. Even Oscar Wilde. He studied the Restoration through a microscope in the morning and repeated it through a telescope in the evening."

"And in *Ulysses*?" I asked.

"They are all there, the great talkers," he answered, "them and the things they forgot. In *Ulysses* I have recorded, simultaneously, what a man says, sees, thinks, and what such seeing, thinking, saying does, to what you Freudians call the subconscious,—but as for psychoanalysis," he broke off, "it's neither more nor less than blackmail."

He raised his eyes. There is something unfocused in them,—the same paleness seen in plants long hidden from the sun,—and sometimes a little jeer that goes with a lift and rounding of the upper lip.

The pitiless and uninterrupted stream rolls by, and its velocity or precipitation grows in the last forty pages till it sweeps away even the marks of punctuation. It thus gives cruelest expression to that emptiness which is both breath taking and stifling, which is under such tension, or is so filled to bursting, as to grow unbearable. This thoroughly hopeless emptiness is the dominant note of the whole book. It not only begins and ends in nothingness, but it consists of nothing but nothingness. It is all infernally nugatory. If we regard the book from the side of technical artistry, it is a positively brilliant and hellish monster-birth. —*C. G. Jung*

For myself then, the pleasure—the very great pleasure—that I get from going through the sentences of Mr. Joyce is that given me simply by the cadence of his prose, and I fancy that the greatest and highest enjoyment that can be got from any writing is simply that given by the cadence of the prose. —*Ford Madox Ford*

A LETTER FROM GEORGE BERNARD SHAW TO SYLVIA BEACH

To you possibly [*Ulysses*] may appeal as art; you are probably (you see I don't know you) a young barbarian beglamoured by the excitements and enthusiasms that art stirs up in passionate material; but to me it is all hideously real: I have walked those streets and know those shops and have heard and taken part in those conversations. I escaped from them to England at the age of twenty; and forty years later have learnt from the books of Mr. Joyce that Dublin is still what it was, and young men are still drivelling in slackjawed blackguardism just as they were in 1870. It is, however, some consolation to find that at last somebody has felt deeply enough about it to face the horror of writing it all down and using his literary genius to force people to face it. In Ireland they try to make a cat cleanly by rubbing its nose in its own filth. Mr. Joyce has tried the same treatment on the human subject. I hope it may prove successful.

EXCERPTS FROM JUDGE WOOLSEY'S DECISION:
United States District Court
Southern District of New York
Opinion A. 110-59

...In writing "Ulysses", Joyce sought to make a serious experiment in a new, if not wholly novel, literary genre. He takes persons of the lower middle class living in Dublin in 1904 and seeks not only to describe what they did on a certain day early in June of that year as they went about the City bent on their usual occupations, but also to tell what many of them thought about the while.

Joyce has attempted—it seems to me, with astonishing success—to show how the screen of consciousness with its ever-shifting kaleidoscopic impressions carries, as it were on a plastic palimpsest, not only what is in the focus of each man's observation of the actual things about him, but also in a penumbral zone residua of past impressions, some recent and some drawn up by association from the domain of the subconscious. He shows how each of these impressions affects the life and behavior of the character which he is describing.

What he seeks to get is not unlike the result of a double or, if that is possible, a multiple exposure on a cinema film which would give a clear foreground with a background visible but somewhat blurred and out of focus in varying degrees.

...The words which are criticized as dirty are old Saxon words known to almost all men and, I venture, to many women, and are such words as would be naturally and habitually used, I believe, by the types of folk whose life, physical and mental, Joyce is seeking to describe. In respect of the recurrent emergence of the theme of sex in the minds of his characters, it must always be remembered that his locale was Celtic and his season Spring.

Whether or not one enjoys such a technique as Joyce uses is a matter of taste on which disagreement or argument is futile, but to subject that technique to the standards of some other technique seems to me to be little short of absurd.

...Furthermore, "Ulysses" is an amazing *tour de force* when one considers the success which has been in the main achieved with such a difficult objective as Joyce set for himself. As I have stated, "Ulysses" is not an easy book to read. It is brilliant and dull, intelligible and obscure by turns. In many places it seems to me to be disgusting, but although it contains, as I have mentioned above, many words usually considered dirty, I have not found anything that I consider to be dirt for dirt's sake. Each word of the book contributes like a bit of mosaic to the detail of the picture which Joyce is seeking to construct for his readers.

If one does not wish to associate with such folk as Joyce describes, that is one's own choice. In order to avoid indirect contact with them one may not wish to read "Ulysses"; that is quite understandable. But when such a real artist in words, as Joyce undoubtedly is, seeks to draw a true picture of the lower middle class in a European city, ought it to be impossible for the American public legally to see that picture?

...I am quite aware that owing to some of its scenes "Ulysses" is a rather strong draught to ask some sensitive, though normal, persons to take. But my considered opinion, after long reflection, is that whilst in many places the effect of "Ulysses" on the reader undoubtedly is somewhat emetic, nowhere does it tend to be an aphrodisiac.

"Ulysses" may, therefore, be admitted into the United States.

John M. Woolsey
United States District Judge
December 6, 1933

...The more we read "Ulysses," the more we are convinced of its psychological truth, and the more we are amazed at Joyce's genius in mastering and in presenting, not through analysis or generalization, but by the complete recreation of life in the process of being lived, the relations of human beings to their environment and to each other; the nature of their perception of what goes on about them and of what goes on within themselves; and the interdependence of their intellectual, their physical, their professional and their emotional lives. To have traced all these interdependences, to have given each of these elements its value, yet never to have lost sight of the moral through preoccupation with the physical, nor to have forgotten the general in the particular; to have exhibited ordinary humanity without either satirizing it or sentimentalizing it—this would already have been sufficiently remarkable; but to have subdued all this material to the uses of a supremely finished and disciplined work of art is a feat which has hardly been equalled in the literature of our time. —*Edmund Wilson*

Joyce in 1904, in the Curran family's garden, Dublin. Ellmann reported in his biography that when Joyce was asked what he was thinking as Constantine Curran photographed him, he replied, "I was wondering would he lend me five shillings."

The Noble Savage of the Novel: Joyce the Artist

2

"The ancient gods, who are visions of the divine names, die and come to life many times, and, though there is dusk about their feet and darkness in their indifferent eyes, the miracle of light is renewed eternally in the imaginative soul." Joyce was twenty, an undergraduate at University College, Dublin, when he wrote these words. In his opinion, Ireland was in a sad state of artistic affairs, and he used his essay on the nineteenth-century poet James Clarence Mangan to elaborate not only on Mangan's art but also on his own aesthetic theories, his ideas on classicism, romanticism, poetry, and art. When read within the context of Joyce's life, his words presage what he would do twenty years later in *Ulysses*. That "the ancient gods are present today" is a claim he spent ten years realizing. In the context of his aesthetic theories, it prophesies his relentless quest for what he believed to be truth in art. "Art is true to itself when it deals with truth....Art is marred by such mistaken insistence on its religious, its moral, its beautiful, its idealizing tendencies." From an early age Joyce demonstrated a fierce idealism, often directed toward the stifling mores of his homeland. In doing so, he exiled himself. He championed the unbound power of the imagination, but it was his self-determination and the will to exercise all of his artistic powers that he cultivated into an indomitable strength. Joyce achieved his first professional publication at the age of eighteen, in the prestigious *Fortnightly Review*, with an essay entitled "Ibsen's New Drama." By the age of forty, he was the most famous living prose writer in the English language. He overcame great obstacles and was strengthened by his belief in his own omnipotence. With "silence, exile and cunning," Joyce disarmed his enemies and never let go of the myth that he was making.

The Joyce Family in 1888. Left to right: Maternal grandfather John Murray, young James, mother Mary Joyce, father John Stanislaus Joyce. Taken on the day James entered Clongowes Wood College. The house is 41 Brighton Square, Rathgar, the house where Joyce was born.

Joyce had known difficulty from an early age. He was the second of ten children who survived, thirteen being one estimate of the number of children his mother bore. His family had fallen, gradually, into poverty, having once enjoyed a middle-class lifestyle. The Irish writer Edna O'Brien, in her biography of James Joyce, gives a snapshot of Joyce's childhood imagery, as he walks, reciting the "silver-veined prose" of the Irish Catholic writer and educator Cardinal Newman "...in an endeavor to banish from his mind the sparring household, the enamel basin in which he had washed himself and the kitchen clock which was one hour and twenty-five minutes fast. His journey led him along the water-logged lanes, past rubbish, offal, dripping trees, corner shops, a stonecutting works that recalled the spirit of his hero Ibsen, and the docks in which the black arms of the tall ships told of distant nations, places he longed to escape to."

"No one who has not lived in such straitened and hideous circumstances can understand the battering of that upbringing," O'Brien remarks.

Although he first left Ireland in 1902 and eventually made his home elsewhere, living in Trieste, Zurich, and Paris, he never escaped. Ireland was the sight on which he set his fierce imagination and the subject of all of Joyce's fiction and most of his writing. His fascination with Ireland is reflected in his recreations, in minutest detail, of the Dublin streets. Throughout his life various themes remained a constant thread in his work: conflict with the Catholic Church; a refusal to succumb to the censorship of literature, a refusal to relinquish his own individuality and the autonomy of his art; admiration for Ibsen and Flaubert; exile; and his relationship to Ireland.

Raised in a religious home, educated by Jesuits, Joyce left the Catholic Church in defiance of its strictures and demands for submission. Upon graduation from university, Joyce left Dublin for Paris. He faced the disappointment of what he considered a failed early career in music, having inherited his father's gift as a tenor. Joyce returned to Dublin in April 1903 after his father sent him a telegram: "MOTHER DYING COME HOME FATHER." As his forty-four-year-old mother lay in a coma in the final stages of life, James and his brother Stanislaus reportedly refused to kneel. The equivalent occurs in *Ulysses* and Buck Mulligan reproaches Stephen for not granting his mother her deathbed wish. James Augustine Joyce chose the confirmation name Aloysius, after the saint who refused to be alone in a room with his mother and feared contact with all women, an interesting detail when viewed within the context of Joyce's own complicated relationships with women. Joyce had been close to his mother and after her death he wandered the streets of Dublin in mourning. In June of 1904, he met Nora Barnacle.

His interest in Nora was obsessive and he expressed his affection in a spectrum of emotions that ranged from exaltation to degradation. He experienced bouts of jealousy that occasionally verged on extreme. Joyce's letters to Nora demonstrate a vast flux from transports of romantic cherishing to the more lewd attentions he paid her, this volatility perhaps a means of keeping a necessary distance, presumably for the protection of his art. Although they shared a love of music among other interests, Nora seemed indifferent to his work. In 1922, when *Ulysses* was published in Paris by Shakespeare and Company, and Joyce gave her an inscribed copy, Nora jokingly threatened to sell the copy he gave her. In Europe, they moved often and the family grew to include two children, Giorgio and Lucia. Lucia suffered mental illness, later diagnosed as schizophrenia, a fact about which Joyce was partially in denial. In spite of Joyce's insistence that Lucia's genius was misdiagnosed as an illness, he took her for many cures. On one occasion C. G. Jung was said to have remarked about Lucia and Joyce that they were like two people going to the bottom of a river, one falling, the other diving.

Throughout his life Joyce maintained close relationships with friends and acquaintances, many of whom are immortalized and some who are satirized in the characters of his fiction. In Europe, Joyce taught but struggled to make money, eventually accepting the aid of various benefactors, including his famous patron Harriet Shaw Weaver, who made great sacrifices for Joyce's art. One of the many paradoxes of Joyce's life was the congeniality he extended to others, the value he placed on family and friendship, and his ability to maintain distance from all who knew him, persevering in his art at all costs. In Paris, Joyce moved in the elite literary circles of the day, still without means, but nonetheless, finding a way to dine well, attend the theatre, and travel. He was a well-known patron of the restaurant Les Trianons, opposite Gare Montparnasse, where the staff kept a table for him in the back. Joyce was fluent in at least five languages, and read four or five newspapers of different nations, daily. While enjoying an exalted life amid the smart set of his day, he suffered illness, poverty, near blindness, censorship, and suppression. Joyce faced daunting financial and health problems while working on *Ulysses*. Between 1917 and 1930 he underwent more than twenty-five eye operations, and often wore a white coat to reflect the available light when he wrote. His book was banned; publishers refused to publish it. He rallied support from friends and acquaintances and continued to accept financial gifts from his patrons.

There was about Joyce an acute awareness, a melancholy solitude, an elegant demeanor, and frequently an aura of arrogance, according to accounts from his contemporaries. This aspect of his character is immortalized in the story of the first meeting between Joyce and Yeats, when Joyce was twenty, and Yeats thirty-six. Joyce is said to have asked Yeats his age. To Yeats's reply he is reported to have said, "I have met you too late. You are too old."

When asked what he thought about life, Joyce is said to have replied, "I don't think about it." He made no distinction between life and literary creation. He emerged from the paralysis of Ireland and invented himself in the image that still inspires interest today. Both the artist and his art remain a puzzle to many and there is no small number of scholars who have devoted their lives to this study. "Beauty, the splendor of truth, is a gracious presence when the imagination contemplates intensely the truth of its own being or the visible world...." This "splendor of truth" was the standard to which he held himself, unfailingly, through poverty, opposition, illness, exile, and unto death. One feels that Joyce is speaking, a priori, of his own difficult and exemplary life when at age twenty, he wrote this line: "In those vast courses which enfold us and in that great memory which is greater and more generous than our memory, no life, no moment of exaltation is ever lost; and all those who have written nobly have not written in vain."

A man of genius makes no mistakes. His errors are volitional and are the portals of discovery. —*James Joyce*

James Joyce, Ezra Pound, John Quinn, and Ford Madox Ford in Paris, Autumn 1923, outside Pound's studio in the rue des Champs.

Such a colossal self-conceit with such a Lilliputian literary genius I never saw combined in one person. —*attributed to W. B. Yeats*

Human society is the embodiment of changeless laws which the whimsicalities and circumstances of men and women involve and overwrap. The realm of literature is the realm of these accidental manners and humours—a spacious realm; and the true literary artist concerns himself mainly with them. —*James Joyce*

As for Joyce, he treated people invariably as his equals, whether they were writers, children, waiters, princesses, or charladies. What anybody had to say interested him; he told me that he had never met a bore. —*Sylvia Beach*

But on the purely personal side, Joyce possesses a good deal of the intolerant arrogance of the dominie, veiled with an elaborate decency beneath the formal calm of the Jesuit, left over as a handy property from his early years of catholic romance—of that Irish variety that is so English that it seems stranger to a continental almost than its English protestant counterpart. —*Wyndham Lewis*

...He had the necessary courage, perseverance, inner strength, and energy of mind—any one of which might easily have been insufficient—to overcome all obstacles, all suffering, and to attain perfection. When his work comes to be judged according to its true value, as posterity will judge it, it will appear overwhelming, if only because of the crushing labour that it obviously represents, and one man's life will seem to have been conceived on too small a scale in comparison with the immensity of the effort involved.
—*Paul Léon*

The most general and lasting impression I shall always retain of Joyce the man is his exquisite gentleness, together with his infinite power of comprehension. By this I do not mean a quality of heart....I am referring to a more general characteristic, one that partakes, as it were, of the elementary forces of his make-up. For gentleness and comprehension, in his case, did not spring from weakness or indifference, but were allied to an inner strength, a directed spiritual activity, such as I have never seen in anyone else.
—*Paul Léon*

...The student of the human soul should read attentively Joyce's writings in which it is mirrored, for Joyce made no distinction between actual life and literary creation. His work is one long self-confession, and in this respect he is akin to the greatest of the romantics. —*Paul Léon*

For at bottom there is in Joyce a profound hatred for humanity—the scholar's hatred. One realizes that he has the neurotic's fear of entering the living world, the world of men and women in which he is powerless to function. He is in revolt not against institutions, but against mankind....*Ulysses* is like a vomit spilled by a delicate child whose stomach has been overloaded with sweetmeats.
—*Henry Miller*

Where the arts were concerned [Joyce] was far from timid. He might have other timidities, might in fact be a curious amalgam of sensitive superstitions and nervous fears, but he was entirely unself-conscious when it came to those profound expressions that were liberated by musical notes and written words. —*Herbert Gorman*

His distraction is comparable only to that legendary kind of certain scholars. People who met him in passing, without observing him and without his noticing them, spoke only of his distraction, some-times calling it egotism. But he was the most affectionate, the most sensitive of friends, and the one who had the greatest impact on me of all those that I have had. —*Philippe Soupault*

His memory was stupendous, but he would go out and withdraw from company, and surely that must have been for note-taking.
—*Oliver St. John Gogarty*

Together we went often to the theatre, which, like all good Irish-men, he loved. It was the theatre as theatre that he loved. I mean that he was attracted less by the play than by the atmosphere, the footlights and spotlights, the spectators, the kind of solemnity in a theatre. He preferred opera. When he had decided to go, he was happy as a child. He chose a companion, refused to dine (I prepare myself for a sacrament, he told me, explaining this abstinence), and after the performance he had supper at a restaurant, where he had arranged to have his favorite white wines. At the theatre, seated in the first row—presumably because of his very bad eyesight—he carefully watched the action and listened closely to the performers. Only children are as passionately attentive as Joyce was.
—*Philippe Soupault*

Joyce met Proust once at a literary dinner, and Proust asked Joyce did he like truffles, and Joyce said yes, he did, and I know Joyce was very amused afterwards. He said "...the two greatest literary figures of our time meet and they ask each other if they like truffles."
—*Arthur Power*

He would never relinquish the anger that he felt then, revolt at the sight of the gray block of Trinity College "set heavily in the city's ignorance," or the statue of Thomas Moore, the national poet, cov-ered in vermin. Even the guileless flower girl entreating him to buy flowers exasperated him and reinforced his fury over his own poverty. No Proustian madeleine would summon up this rigorous landscape. For him, as Auden would say of Yeats, "Mad Ireland hurt you into poetry." —*Edna O'Brien*

Jim says that he writes well because when he writes his mind is as nearly normal as possible. —*Stanislaus Joyce*

James Joyce, photographed by Berenice Abbott, Paris, 1926.

No one to my knowledge has subjugated his life to his work more
completely than James Joyce did. —*Philippe Soupault*

PAUL LÉON: IN MEMORY OF JOYCE

The following excerpt is from an unsigned letter from Paul Léon to Jean Paulhan, publisher of the Nouvelle Revue Française, *written four months after Joyce's death. Léon had been Joyce's friend and de facto assistant in Paris. The letter, which has been translated by Maria Jolas, was unsigned so as not to attract the attention of the German authorities.*

I recall a day in late September 1930. I was leaving for a holiday and Joyce had insisted on walking with me part of the way towards the Gare de Lyon. I am a very poor walker, just the opposite of Joyce, and our strolls aroused in me only moderate enthusiasm. I believe, however, that he felt safer crossing the streets when I held his arm. But the two of us must have made a sorry pair in the streets of Paris and, in fact, Philippe Soupault had baptized us "the halt and the blind." That day, as we walked quietly along the Boulevard Raspail, Joyce was suddenly stopped by a young girl who, somewhat awkwardly but charmingly, complimented him on his work. Joyce lifted his unfortunate eyes towards the still-sunny sky, then brought them back to the boxed trees growing along the Boulevard: "You would do better," he said to the girl, "to admire the sky or even these poor trees." Should that young girl chance to read these lines, she will perhaps recognize herself, but I should like [her] to know how great a truth lay behind this apparently banal suggestion. This was not false modesty, but a genuine admiration for the natural universe; for its colours which he could hardly distinguish, but which he appreciated all the more fully in consequence; for the constant mobility of its forms, whether pleasing or unshapely; for its sounds, to which only recently we listened together, stretched out on the grass in the Allier; for the human beings who people and quicken it with their thoughts, their passions, whether good or evil, noble or base, harmonious or discordant.

I see him again, during one of the days I spent with him, tortured by a word, almost rebelliously constructing a framework, questioning his characters, extracting a vision from some music, throwing himself exhaustedly on a couch, the better to hear that phrase which was about to be born, about to burst into light. Then for an hour or more a deep silence, broken by laughs. —*Philippe Soupault*

His influence, however, is local. Like Synge, another Irish writer, he has had his day. —*Gertrude Stein*

———

To call this man angry is too temperate a word, he was volcanic. —*Edna O'Brien*

———

He would carry his work "like a chalice" and all his life he would insist that what he did "was a kind of sacrament." Father, Son and Holy Ghost along with Jakes McCarthy informed every graven word. On a more secular note he liked blackberry jam because Christ's crown of thorns came from that wood and he wore purple cravats during Lent. —*Edna O'Brien*

———

Joyce at that time [while at university] was a slim and elegant young man, with very blue eyes, thin lips, rather square chin, forehead, as he carried his head always very, in almost an arrogant fashion, with his chin pushed out. A very graceful carriage. —*Constantine Curran*

———

Looking back, there was something uncanny in his certainty, which he had more than any other writer I have ever known, that he would one day be famous. It was more than mere wishful thinking. It governed all his attitudes to his compatriots and accounts for what many referred to as his arrogance. He was never really arrogant, but seemed to have a curious sense of his own powers and wouldn't tolerate anyone who didn't really appreciate his work. —*Oliver St. John Gogarty*

———

Joyce did not write about his agony, he lived it. —*Louis Gillet*

I don't know whether or not my husband is a genius, but I'm sure of one thing, there is no one like him. —*Nora Joyce*

Nora Barnacle and James Joyce on their wedding day, July 4, 1931, accompanied by their solicitor. The couple had eloped in 1904.

... I will try to express myself in my art as freely as I can and wholly as I can, using for my defense the only arms I allow myself to use, silence, exile and cunning. —*James Joyce*

Cartoon of Joyce and his friends, by F. Scott Fitzgerald, 1928.

JAMES JOYCE AND NEUCHÂTEL

According to his friend Siegfried Giedion, Joyce was a devotee of Swiss wines, much to the dismay of his French friends. On hearing that Joyce's favorite wine was Neuchâtel, a connoisseur, Lettie Teague, wine editor of Food & Wine, *shared this insight:*

I don't know anyone who drinks Swiss wine. Or talks about Swiss wine. Or buys or sells Swiss wine. Swiss chocolates yes, Watches, of course. But not wine. Swiss wine is expensive and hard to find—its best quality is said to be an agreeable neutrality. So when I read that James Joyce was a big fan of Swiss wine, specifically those made in the Neuchâtel region, I was taken aback. What could the author of *Ulysses* and *Finnegans Wake* have found in such wines? I decided to investigate. So I bought a bottle of a good Neuchâtel. It was certainly a pleasant enough drink—crisp and clean but completely forgettable. Perhaps that was the secret: A great writer could be too distracted by an equally great wine.

What is better than to sit at the end of the day and drink wine with friends, or with substitutes for friends? I say at the end of the day, for I would not drink wine until the sun goes down. Wine is sunshine; under the figure of wine the Creator of the Universe could manifest himself. Can you imagine a manifestation under another figure? —*James Joyce*

———

I remember James Joyce as a regular visitor to the Library during the years 1899 to 1904.... he was a tall willowy young man, dressed in a double-breasted reefer jacket, and with a blue yachting cap. He was rather given to striking poses, and would sometimes stand at the desk staring around him at the other people in the waiting-room. —*Francis Blake, attendant, National Library of Ireland*

———

He started and seemed very apprehensive when he heard a little dog barking in the garden. He said, "I'm very much afraid of dogs, you know, since one bit me when I was five years old, and I had a scar on the chin and that's why I wear this slight beard." In fact he had a little goatee. —*Sylvia Beach*

———

Joyce exhibited a character trait so common among Irishmen that it could be called the Irish paradox—faithfulness to one woman and at the same time a profound hostility toward women in general. This may be due to the Puritanism which exists in Irish Catholicism. ...It would be interesting to determine whether the coldness, the bigotry, and the absolute lack of romance in Irish women are innate or whether they are unconsciously desired by the males of the race; for, in the final analysis, women are always blamed for being what men themselves desire them to be. —*Stanislaus Joyce*

Endowed with a Rabelaisian ability for word invention, embittered by the domination of a church for which his intellect had no use, harassed by the lack of understanding on the part of family and friends, obsessed by the parental image against which he vainly rebels, Joyce has been seeking escape in the erection of a fortress composed of meaningless verbiage. His language is a ferocious masturbation carried on in fourteen tongues. —*Henry Miller*

His last words were, 'Does nobody understand?'—and I'm afraid that's what none of us did—understand him. —*Eva Joyce*

THE OBITUARY OF JAMES JOYCE
Irish Independent, *January 13, 1941*

James Joyce, the famous Irish-born writer, died in hospital in Zurich at 2:15 a.m. today. He was 58.

Though he was pronounced out of danger earlier yesterday, his condition became worse last night. Blood transfusions were given at once. On Saturday he had undergone an emergency abdominal operation.

James Joyce was one of the most discussed figures in contemporary literature.

Born on 2nd February 1882, he was educated at Clongowes Wood and later at Belvedere and took his B.A. degree at the Royal University.

Even as a university student he became known as a writer and he was regarded as one of the most brilliant students of his generation.

His chief publications before he went to live on the Continent were his collection of short stories, *Dubliners*, and his semi-autobiographical work *A Portrait of the Artist as a Young Man*.

Opinions about his later work vary, but there is a general agreement that those two books were notable contributions to English literature and that they showed great imagination, a fine use of words, an extraordinary sensitiveness to the social, political and religious life of the Dublin of the day. When he left Ireland not long before the 1914–18 war, he went first to

Trieste, as a teacher, and later lived in Rome and Zurich before settling in Paris. His chief works of the Continental period were *Ulysses* and *Work in Progress* [*Finnegans Wake*], the latter published in fragment.

By that time he had changed his whole idea of writing. It might even be said that he had changed his whole idea of language. Those latter publications were written in a language that the ordinary reader would recognise only here and there as English.

He had become hostile to the Catholic Church, in which he had been brought up. But in all his writings it seems as if he were never easy about his attitude to the Church, as if his quarrel with it preyed on his mind continually.

Visitors to him in Paris of late years have spoken of him as always being very much interested in news of Dublin and very fond of talking about his native city. They have described him as usually being dressed in white, and finding it necessary, owing to his failing sight, to write with a great red pencil on huge sheets of paper.

His last book, *Work in Progress*, was published about a year ago, though he had begun to work on it as far back as 1923.

He married Nora, daughter of Thomas Barnacle, of Galway, in 1904. They had one son and one daughter.

Ezra Pound at the grave of James Joyce, Zurich, 1967.

A first edition copy of Ulysses, *published in 1922 by Shakespeare and Company in Paris. This copy was owned by Maurice Darantiere, the French printer of the book.*

The Epic of the Age: Themes of *Ulysses*

3

In November 1933, the controversy over *Ulysses* intensified as Random House fought in the U.S. District Court of Southern New York for the right to publish the book. *Ulysses* was ruled to be obscene under Section 305 of the Tariff Act of 1930, Title 19 United States Code, Section 1305, and for that reason, it was argued, should not be imported into the United States and, in addition, should be subject to seizure, forfeiture, confiscation, and destruction. Judge John Woolsey presided. On December 6, 1933, Woolsey ruled that *Ulysses* was not obscene and the landmark decision cleared the way for legal publication and sale of the novel in the United States.

"Thus one half of the English speaking world surrenders. The other half will follow.... And Ireland 1000 years hence," Joyce reportedly remarked at the news.

In spite of the presence of "dirty" words, Woolsey found no evidence in *Ulysses* of anything that he deemed "dirt for dirt's sake." Additionally, Judge Woolsey enumerated the qualities he found admirable and his insightful articulations championed Joyce's cause. In describing *Ulysses*, he called it a "true picture." He referred to the "screen of consciousness with its ever-shifting kaleidoscopic impressions," to the subconscious, and to multiple exposures in cinematic film. He suggested that Joyce had evolved a new literary genre...."*Ulysses* is an amazing *tour de force* when one considers the success which has been in the main achieved with such a difficult objective as Joyce set for himself." Woolsey speculated on Joyce's motives: "Accordingly, I hold that *Ulysses* is a sincere and honest book and I think that the criticisms of it are entirely disposed of by its rationale."

Ulysses exceeds seven hundred pages in length but its subject is one day in Dublin. That Joyce took the classical text of Homer's *Odyssey* and transposed it with the trappings of daily life in early twentieth-century Dublin, giving epic proportion to a prosaic day in Dublin, is a feat unto itself. That he set himself the task of writing a book from eighteen different points of view and in as many styles is impressive. But more than anything, in portraying man, the ultimate everyman, and depicting life in its richest detail; the mundane, the ordinary, the spectacular; the history of the English language—in a work of fiction whose facets refract simultaneously all that is most human—Joyce surpassed what had been done before in the English novel.

"The only thing that interests me is style," Joyce reportedly said. He referred to interior monologue as the stylization of consciousness. "From my point of view, it hardly matters whether the technique is 'veracious' or not; it has served me as a bridge over which to march my eighteen episodes, and, once I have got my troops across, the opposing forces can, for all I care, blow the bridge sky-high."

In *Ulysses*, Joyce eschews action in favor of the psychological portrait. There is no plot and multiple perspectives propel the narrative. Joyce relied on epiphanies, symbols, images, impressions, and dreams for meaning. By telescoping and fragmenting time, the presentation of experience becomes layered, allusive, discontinuous. Through the use of a transformational language, stream of consciousness, free association, interior monologue, and montage, Joyce constructed a new reality of time and space: contracting and expanding, kaleidoscopic and hallucinatory. With the invention of photography in the mid-nineteenth century, the world gained access to a new visual language. In capturing $1/125$ of a second, the photograph isolated aspects of temporality that exist in the fractional moment. Time and space were interrupted, fixed, enlarged, or reduced. Motion pictures, the automobile, and the radio subsequently opened the realm of the senses to new experiences, while World War I, with its mechanized killing, shattered the moral underpinnings of European society. By the end of the war the age of romanticism had ended—industry, science, psychology were the new gods, and for Joyce and many of his contemporaries, aesthetics outranked ethics.

Ulysses opens with Stephen Dedalus and Buck Mulligan in a game of intellectual sparring and establishes an authorial strategy. Joyce was working with and against all that had preceded him, in full control of the elements he employed. His model in youth was Ibsen, whose restraint he would imitate, and then work against. Moving beyond his nineteenth-century predecessors, James and Flaubert, Joyce used what had already been done to establish a new narrative style. He borrowed from religion; his epiphanies imbued the eucharistic with secular meaning. He juxtaposed the high and

James Joyce's sketch of his character Leopold Bloom.

the low. He used vividness, which he understood as the inclusion of all detail, a tenet of Greek literary style. With heroic and mythic allusions he ennobled the commonplace, and in inserting himself into an ancient tale, Joyce transformed its qualities into a modern myth.

Joyce is often considered a pioneer of modernism, but by the time Joyce was writing *Ulysses*, the methods of narrative representation had already changed radically. By the turn of the century, Joseph Conrad had begun to experiment with the form of the novel. For Conrad and others there was no new story to tell; invention resided in method. In Conrad's *Heart of Darkness*, published in 1899, story is a vehicle for personal impressions, a recording of experiences of an interior and highly psychological nature. His innovations of story structure served as provenance for such writers as Joyce, William Faulkner, and Ernest Hemingway. Other core modernist writers of fiction in English include Ford Madox Ford, D. H. Lawrence, and Virginia Woolf. Modernism in poetry is often associated with the publication of T. S. Eliot's "The Love Song of J. Alfred Prufrock" in 1917. The year 1922 saw the publication of Joyce's *Ulysses* and Eliot's *The Waste Land*. By 1933, the time of Woolsey's decision, Virginia Woolf had written *The Waves*.

Joyce said of *Ulysses*: "It is the epic of two races (Israel-Ireland) and at the same time the cycle of the human body as well as a little story of a day (life). The character of Ulysses always fascinated me ever since boyhood. I started writing it as a short story for *Dubliners* fifteen years ago but gave it up. For seven years I have been working at this book—blast it!"

As Beckett remarks, "Literary criticism is not bookkeeping....The danger is in the neatness of identifications." *Ulysses* defies easy categorization. It's been called a spiritual autobiography and a *Bildungsroman*. In the eight decades since its publication, scholars, academics, literary critics, and readers around the world continue to argue the points and details of *Ulysses*. That *Ulysses* has achieved such fame is no accident. It was Joyce's intention that *Ulysses* be enigmatic, and close study reveals an intricate plan that Joyce devised to keep the scholars busy. He chose not to challenge interpretations, he allowed the controversies to speak for themselves, and in his own silent and cunning way, he encouraged the modern mythic proportions of *Ulysses*. Joyce created Leopold Bloom in the image of the Homeric hero, but he created a piece of literature in which he revealed himself and humanity, documenting a single, eternal, fictional day in more than seven hundred pages.

You should approach Joyce's *Ulysses* as the illiterate Baptist preacher approaches the Old Testament: with faith.
—*William Faulkner*

I was on the platform, my heart going like the locomotive, as the train from Dijon came slowly to a standstill and I saw the conductor getting off, holding a parcel and looking around for someone—me. In a few minutes, I was ringing the doorbell at the Joyces' and handing them Copy No. 1 of *Ulysses*. It was February 2, 1922.
—*Sylvia Beach*

Joyce has attempted in "Ulysses" to render as exhaustively, as precisely and as directly as it is possible in words to do, what our participation in life is like—or rather, what it seems to us like as from moment to moment we live. —*Edmund Wilson*

I want to give a picture of Dublin so complete that if the city one day suddenly disappeared from the earth it could be reconstructed out of my book. —*James Joyce*

Joyce has a most goddamn wonderful book. —*Ernest Hemingway*

"Ulysses" creates the illusion of a living social organism. We see it only for twenty hours, yet we know its past as well as its present. We possess Dublin, seen, heard, smelt, and felt, brooded over, imagined, remembered. —*Edmund Wilson*

The whole of *Ulysses*, as we shall gradually realize, is a deliberate pattern of recurrent themes and synchronization of trivial events. —*Vladimir Nabokov*

The Custom House in Dublin, beside Custom House Quay on the River Liffey, 1885.

If it be urged that Joyce's gift for fantasy is attested by the superb drunken scene, I reply that this scene is successful, not because it is reckless nonsense but because it is an accurate record of drunken states of mind. —*Edmund Wilson*

If you were ever flushed and excited by *Ulysses* you are probably now over forty; if you ever tried to live by it, over thirty. Under thirty, people seem to be a little bored by Joyce's endless experimentation, and also by the setting up of a polarity between prose and poetry which is rendered in terms of straight talk about the genitals or swooning pre-Raphaelite rhythms. —*Frank Kermode*

If I gave it all up immediately, I'd lose my immortality. I've put in so many enigmas and puzzles that it will keep the professors busy for centuries arguing over what I meant, and that's the only way of insuring one's immortality. —*James Joyce*

Ulysses is a splendid and permanent structure, but it has been slightly overrated by the kind of critic who is more interested in ideas and generalities and human aspects than in the work of art itself. —*Vladimir Nabokov*

...In Bloom's mind and in Joyce's book the theme of sex is continually mixed and intertwined with the theme of the latrine.
—*Vladimir Nabokov*

What stimulates him is *ways of doing things*, and technical processes, and not *things to be done*. —*Wyndham Lewis*

EXCERPT FROM "A REPORT ON FOUR WRITERS OF THE MODERN PSYCHOLOGICAL SCHOOL"

A term report by Tennessee Williams, undergraduate

...Speaking of *Ulysses*, there is, in the first place, much too much of it. There are 768 pages of small, close type with an almost maximum economy of punctuation and indentation. Obviously Mr. Joyce set out to produce a monumental piece of work and was determined that it should be monumental in every sense of the word. It is the most deliberately pretentious work of art I have ever come across. It would seem doomed at the start to be either a colossal failure [or] a colossal success but somehow or other it doesn't seem to be exactly either. Mr. Joyce does not quite accomplish his object, in my opinion. He has made a tremendous effort and yet fallen short of his mark. You have to respect him for having been very earnest and uncompromising about what he was trying to do. He could have given the book a sugar-coating that would have made it much easier to swallow and would have obviated a lot of trouble with the Purity League. But Mr. Joyce was determined that everything Mr. Bloom thought of doing or doing should be accurately and specifically read into the record. He wanted to give us Mr. Bloom. The whole Bloom and nothing but Mr. Bloom. The question in my mind is this: Was Mr. Bloom worth the trouble? I don't think so.

Mr. Bloom is a credible but utterly repugnant creature. He has the nauseous nastiness of a nasty small boy. He is a small-minded, sensual, viciously uxorious, middle-aged Hebrew. He is not a representative character. He is not representative of his race nor of any class of people. Why did Mr. Joyce select such a character to build his novel around? The answer seems to be that Mr. Joyce has a gift for analyzing obscenity and Mr. Bloom supplied the most suitable foil for the exposition of that gift.

The story has no plot. In fact it is not a story. It is just a record of a man's consciousness during a single day and night: what goes on in his mind as he goes about his trivial, dull affairs. The consciousness is mostly Mr. Bloom's, though it is sometimes varied with that of lesser characters, notably Mrs. Bloom (in the closing soliloquy) and Stephen Dedalus, a young teacher.

...A great deal of dullness. Then some dirt. Then more dullness. Then a great deal more dirt and a great deal more dullness. That is my impression of most of *Ulysses*.

...Nymphs, witches, figures, bells, jurors, nameless ones, quoits, watches, a crier, recorder, elector, chimes, gramophone, sundry whores, the end of the world, Zoefanny, Virag, Bello, Sleepy Hollow and Old Gummy Granny are a few of the quaint characters who take a more or less meaningless part in this jamboree [of the Nighttown section]. It is the one thoroughly unintelligible section of the book. It may be excusable as representation of a drunken state of mind. But if anybody got that drunk I think recovery would be out of the question.

...Mrs. Bloom's soliloquy which makes up the remainder of the book is decidedly its best portion. It Is an astonishingly keen analysis of a woman's character. A very low sort of character but more colorful and interesting than Bloom's. She also has a streak of tenderness and some appreciation of beauty which make her reflections more readable (though quite as lascivious) as her husband's.

I think the book would be a more creditable performance, on the whole, if Mrs. Bloom's soliloquy was left to stand by itself. It is the supreme exposition of Mr. Joyce's method and it is the only part of the book, frankly, which I found worth reading.

Each chapter, where not one false note, not one error, not one thing to regret is discernable, forms so definitive an ensemble that even an inattentive or uncertain reader cannot escape a spell that he is completely incapable of explaining or throwing off. Joyce extracts from his reader an effort which cannot be dispersed. He first imposes on him his tone, his color, his style. The imagination is never allowed free rein. From the first word, he who dares to begin reading is as though seized, and cost what it may, he must submit himself to the will of the author. It is a test of strength.
—*Philippe Soupault*

I am quite aware that owing to some of its scenes "Ulysses" is a rather strong draught to ask some sensitive, though normal, persons to take. But my considered opinion, after long reflection, is that whilst in many places the effect of "Ulysses" on the reader undoubtedly is somewhat emetic, nowhere does it tend to be an aphrodisiac. "Ulysses" may, therefore, be admitted into the United States. —*Judge John M. Woolsey*

I hold *Ulysses* to be the most important expression which the present age has found; it is a book to which we are all indebted, and from which none of us can escape. —*T. S. Eliot*

The action takes place in one day...in a single place, Dublin. Telemachus wanders *beside the shore of the loud and roaring sea*; he sees the midwives with their professional bags. Ulysses breakfasts, circulates; mass, funeral, bath house, race tracktalk; the other characters circulate; the soap circulates; he hunts for advertising, the "ad" of the House of Keyes, he visits the national library to verify an anatomical detail of mythology, he comes to the isle of Aeolus (a newspaper office), all the noises burst forth, tramways, trucks, post office wagons, etc.; Nausicaä appears, they dine at the hospital; the meeting of Ulysses and Telemachus, the brothel, the brawl, the return to Bloom's, and then the author presents Penelope, symbol of the earth, whose night thoughts end the story as counterweight to the ingenuities of the male. —*Ezra Pound*

This novel belongs to that large class of novels in sonata form, that is to say, in the form: theme, counter-theme, recapitulation, development, finale. And in the subdivision: father and son novel. —*Ezra Pound*

Only Chaucer's Wife of Bath can rival Molly in her frank and wildly humorous evaluation of men. —*Edna O'Brien*

Ulysses, of course, is a divine work of art and will live on despite the academic nonentities who turn it into a collection of symbols or Greek myths. I once gave a student a C-minus, or perhaps a D-plus, just for applying to its chapters the titles borrowed from Homer while not even noticing the comings and goings of the man in the brown mackintosh. He didn't even know who the man in the brown mackintosh was. Oh, yes, let people compare me to Joyce by all means, but my English is pat ball to Joyce's champion game. —*Vladimir Nabokov*

Ulysses can be read with passion without intellectually understanding the text. In this case, we identify ourselves completely with the character, our imagination lays hold of his sensation, his pleasure, his reminiscences, and we live with him, we dream with him. The prolonging of the interior monologue in our imagination will provoke pure reverie.... Because the interior monologue in its fragmentary incoherence includes, as we have seen before, all the logical structure and grammatical armature of thought. —*Emeric Fischer*

The incredible multifariousness of Joyce's style has a monotonous and hypnotic effect. Nothing comes to the reader; everything turns away from him and leaves him to gape after it. The book is always up and away; it is not at peace with itself but is at once ironic, sarcastic, poisonous, disdainful, sad, despairing, and bitter. —*C. G. Jung*

If the later writing of Joyce is read aloud it greatly gains. One realises the sense of strange words. —*Sisley Huddleston*

———

I had an old uncle whose thinking was always to the point. One day he stopped me on the street and asked, "Do you know how the devil tortures the souls in hell?" When I said no, he declared, "He keeps them waiting." And with that he walked away. This remark occurred to me when I was ploughing through *Ulysses* for the first time. Every sentence raises an expectation which is not fulfilled; finally, out of sheer resignation, you come to expect nothing any longer. Then bit by bit, again to your horror, it dawns upon you that in all truth you have hit the nail on the head. It is actual fact that nothing happens and nothing comes of it, and yet a secret expectation at war with hopeless resignation drags the reader from page to page. —*C. G. Jung*

———

The only demand I make of my reader is that he should devote his whole life to reading my works. —*James Joyce*

———

The main contents of the book [*Ulysses*] are enough to make a Hottentot sick...not alone sordidly pornographic, but intensely dull. —*Attributed to a correspondent in* The Sporting Times*, 1922*

———

After the closing picture of Molly Bloom a-dreaming on her dirty bed we can say, as in Revelation—And there shall be no more curse! Henceforth no sin, no guilt, no fear, no repression, no longing, no pain of separation. The end is accomplished—man returns to the womb. —*Henry Miller*

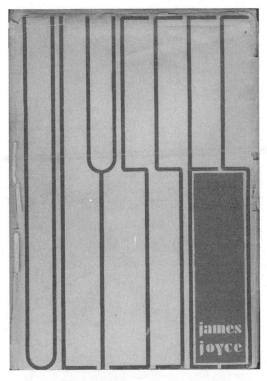

Jacket of the 1934 Random House edition of Ulysses, *the first to be legally published in the United States.*

"Joyce" on stilts, in Dublin on Bloomsday, 2003.

Bloomsday Around the World

4

In a notebook of June 1924 Joyce made mention of the twentieth anniversary of the day *Ulysses* takes place. At the time, Joyce was recovering from a fifth eye surgery and on June 16 he received a bouquet of hydrangeas from friends in honor of "Bloomsday." His notebook contains this entry: "Today, 16 of June 1924 twenty years after. Will anybody remember this date." Sylvia Beach, Joyce's publisher in Paris, is said to have coined the term *Bloomsday* and she continued to host yearly gatherings throughout the 1920s. In 1929, Joyce and company traveled by bus to a village outside Paris for a lively luncheon hosted by the bookseller Adrienne Monnier, at the Hotel Leopold. The day was doubly momentous, marking the French translation of *Ulysses* and the twenty-fifth anniversary of Bloomsday. The story goes that the party returned to Paris via several stops for drink, and Samuel Beckett, who insisted on continuing the imbibitions, was eventually left behind.

Fifty years after the fictional date, a gathering of five individuals instigated the first Bloomsday celebration in Dublin on record. Brian O'Nolan, a writer for the *Irish Times*, the poet Patrick Kavanagh, the young critic Anthony Cronin, a dentist named Tom Joyce (a cousin of James Joyce), and John Ryan, a painter and businessman who owned and edited a literary magazine, set out in a horse-drawn cab from Dublin to Sandycove. Each member assumed the identities of certain characters as they began their journey, intending to tour all the sites of *Ulysses* but eventually succumbing to the safety of the Bailey, a pub on Duke Street, run by John Ryan. Thus began the tradition of Bloomsday.

By the 1980s Bloomsday sightings were reported in many cities around the world. One hundred years later, June 16 is an international celebration—a secular day of semireligious obligation. As the centenary arrives the celebrations have grown to global proportions. Although Bloomsday is a single day, the 2004 festivities will last a bit longer. On June 16 the revelry goes on from dawn to dusk across the globe in more than sixty cities where *Ulysses* is read in more than a dozen languages. From Tokyo to Melbourne, San Francisco to Buffalo, Dublin to Trieste, the celebrations include carnivalesque reenactments and streetside improvisations of scenes from the novel. Dublin is the heart of the party, and hosts a lavish celebration in situ, as it were—in the hometown of Molly and Leopold Bloom, Stephen Dedalus, Buck Mulligan, Gerty MacDowell, and James Joyce himself. From a breakfast of kidneys to a lunch of cheese and wine, to a funeral, to a brothel, Bloomsday entails much celebration for Joyce enthusiasts—novice, academic, or Bloomsday regular alike—as *Ulysses* maintains both intellectual and popular appeal. On stages around the world and in the street, in pubs and public spaces, singing, dancing, and readings take place and it is a joyous rite of springtime. The novel brings together people of all countries, the Irish, the Catholics, the Jewish, lovers of language, of literature, and everyone has something to contribute. When read out loud, one can hear the music, and rereading offers the chance to go deeper, each time finding a new discovery and adding new dimensions to this annual celebration of life.

Dublin, Ireland

It is only fitting that Joyce's native city should be home to the most elaborate Bloomsday festival of all. Dublin was host to the first Bloomsday in 1954—the revels of the group of five whose stamina was no match for their good intentions. Since then Dublin has been host to thousands on Bloomsday. For the 2004 centennial, the depth and breadth expand to maximum proportions with five months of events across the entire city.

The inaugural event is the James Joyce Centre's annual birthday lecture, launching the springtime lecture series. The February 2 lecture provides a forum for discussion and a wealth of educational perspectives on the Irish author. The program includes short courses and lunchtime talks providing the general public with a clear, concise overview of Joyce's life and works. Other events include street theatre, art exhibitions, music programs, and dramatic readings.

"ReJoyce Dublin," a five-month Bloomsday festival lasting from April 1 to August 31, is targeted at the entire spectrum of revelers, from the merely curious to Joyce scholars. The celebration culminates with two breakfasts, one on O'Connell Street, with ten thousand expected, and the Guinness breakfast, hosted by the James Joyce Centre.

Around town there will be a variety of walking tours, each exploring Joyce's life and work from a different theme or perspective, while bus tours will wind through the current Joycean landscape. (The years since 1904 have made an exact replica of Bloom's route impossible. Bloom's home at 7 Eccles Street no longer exists, and

Denizens of Nighttown celebrate Bloomsday in Dublin, 2000.

the red-light district, Nighttown, in which the hallucinatory "Circe" episode takes place, has been leveled.)

Dublin always hosts spectacular exhibitions and events for Bloomsday, including bike rallies and vintage car shows. Every year many people arrive in horse-drawn carriages wearing candy-striped blazers and flowing skirts, bowlers and boaters, watch chains and parasols. There is surely no better day to be in this celebrated city than June 16, when the spirit of *Ulysses* returns, larger than life.

James Joyce Centre
35 North Great Georges Street
Dublin 1, Ireland

Tel: 3531-8788547
E-mail: admin@jamesjoyce.ie
www.rejoycedublin2004.com

Bloomsday in Dublin used to be seen as purely for tourists or academics. Over the past six years we have been trying to change that by taking it to the streets, to the city, where it belongs, whether it is readings for rush-hour commuters in Westland Row Station or performances for lunching office workers in Temple Bar Square. Thankfully this is working; last year we had seven hundred people having breakfast on North Great George's Street enjoying readings, performances, and music, and most of them were Dubliners. Of course, visitors are very welcome and many thousands are expected in 2004, including groups representing Bloomsday celebrations in Europe, Australia, and America who are coming to Dublin to participate in our festival and mark the centenary in the city where it all began. —*Helen Monaghan, Director, James Joyce Centre, and grand-niece of James Joyce*

Bloomsday in Dublin has changed immensely since I became curator of the James Joyce Museum in 1978, from an occasion of somewhat esoteric enjoyment to a city-paralyzing street party. For me, however, fixed at the omphalos, the annual rituals remain constant: the rising at six o'clock, the bicycle ride to Sandycove, the early swim at the Forty Foot, the donning of the ceremonial suit, the local breakfast, the raising of the flag and opening of the Tower at eight o'clock, the arrival of the hundreds and multitudes (annual regulars, newcomers, groups, journalists, and the odd celebrity), the rooftop readings in the sunshine, the crowds on the staircase, the escape at the end of the day for dinner with other survivors from the James Joyce Institute, and rounding up the night with the greatest entertainers of them all, the Balloonatics. I may not see much of Bloomsday, but I see the best of it. —*Robert Nicholson, Curator, James Joyce Museum*

A couple of years ago we were reenacting as usual the funeral of Paddy Dignam from the "Hades" episode of *Ulysses*. The cortege set off with Bob Joyce (the grandnephew of James Joyce) sitting on the box with the driver and his brother Derek impersonating Mr. Dignam inside the box. By the time they got to Cross Guns Bridge, the coffin had become stuffy and, when the cortege stopped at the traffic lights, Derek lifted the lid and had a look around to see how much further they had to go. A party of schoolchildren in an adjoining bus fainted. Thinking this hilarious the jarvey hit the horse a crack at the backside and the hearse took off. However, overcome by hilarity, they took a corner in the graveyard too rapidly, the hearse turned over, the jarvey sustained contusions and abrasions of various kinds and Bob Joyce broke his ankle. The only person to survive unscathed was the "corpse." A truly Joycean outcome. —*Senator David Norris*

Symphony Space, New York, New York

"Bloomsday on Broadway," under the artistic direction of Isaiah Sheffer, is the largest Bloomsday celebration in the United States. The finest actors of stage and screen assemble in the backstage "Barney Kiernan's Tavern" on the famous day, to go over their lines and sip from the locally legendary McSorley's stash if so inclined. Rumor has it that one year, as the revelers warmed up, the sounds backstage rivaled those onstage.

Each year, Isaiah and his team, including Caraid O'Brien, along with the Symphony Space staff, choose a theme such as "Paternity" or "A Whirlwind Tour of *Ulysses*" (see introduction). There's a casual lunch of Gorgonzola and wine, and the reading continues into the wee hours, when, traditionally, the esteemed actress Fionnula Flanagan or another bright star reads Molly's soliloquy. If you run into Isaiah, he likes to recall the time he assembled eleven women of different nationalities on stage for the finale, savoring the international sounds of "yes" and the audience's applause at the final "Da, da, da."

Symphony Space
2537 Broadway
New York, NY 10025-6990
Tel: 212-864-1414
E-mail: info@symphonyspace.org
www.symphonyspace.org

The day I really felt that I was a New Yorker was the day Isaiah [Sheffer] called and asked me to be part of Bloomsday for the first time. And I still wait eagerly each year to see if there is a place for me in the run-up to Fionnula's Molly. My first introduction to *Ulysses* and to Molly Bloom was when my family bought a paperback copy of the photography book *The Family of Man* and there in it was the sexiest photo I'd ever seen—a young Irish couple in a park kissing and underneath, the caption "yes I said yes I will Yes"—ravished then and ravished I remain. —*Kathleen Chalfant*

On Bloomsday, we are Joyce's puppets as we willingly surrender ourselves to his world. Only from the mind of an egomaniacal Irishman could such a holiday be created. —*Caraid O'Brien*

Bloomsday is an oasis where actors can slake their thirst for great material, stretch their minds alongside fellow Joyceans.
—*Barbara Feldon*

Bloomsday on Broadway—what a wonderful experience it was for me, twice over, cohosting with the matchless Isaiah Sheffer two marathon readings of Joyce's *Ulysses* and Homer's *Odyssey*. Back and forth we went between Homer and Joyce, episode by episode, the ancient masterwork illuminating the modern, the modern rejuvenating the fine old bones of Homer. And all of it read aloud—just as it should be—performed by the marvelous troupe of actors whom Isaiah mustered for the occasion. It was Homer and Joyce as I'd always hoped to hear them: as the two comrades-in-arms they really are. —*Robert Fagles*

Bloomsday was always celebrated in my family. My father, Gilbert Seldes, was one of the first American critics to write about *Ulysses* (in *The Nation*, August 30, 1922) and later came to know James Joyce. Many years later, I joined the Joyce Society that met at the Gotham Book Mart in New York. Then came Symphony Space! The connection of Joyce's words with the readers and the audience is magical. I love being a part of it. —*Marian Seldes*

And don't I fondly recall those bygone Bloomsdays, 'ere the Symphony Space was all gussied up and lah di dah and who gave a damn if you spilled a drop on the carpet, not Sheffer, I'm sure, so long as you keep the noise down, friends, and wasn't Guinness a sponsor back then, and Mr. Jameson and Mr. Bushmill as well, I think, and wasn't there plenty consumed by the zealots, the nitpickingreadersalong, the audience, that is, and maybe more by the artistes themselves, and doesn't it go without saying that amongst such a troupe of seasoned, not to say salted and pickled, professionals that said consumption did not, did not, I say did not detract from articulation and dramatic irony, although the pauses are always a problem on the radio, and in many cases, weren't the renderings greatly, ornately enhanced by the booze, excepting, of course, that time when, oh Jesus, that time when McCourt (M.)...ah well, that'll do. To hell with it.
—*Stephen "O'" Lang (soberly)*

Last year on Bloomsday, I dressed in my theatre as Bloom, in a black mourning suit, black bowler, and portmanteau before jumping on the No. 1 train to head uptown to Symphony Space. I was a celebrity. On the train people would come up to me and ask shyly, "You're Bloom, aren't you?" and I would nod "yes." Everyone was delighted to see me, they were looking for me, their literary pop star, and out on the street, they called to me, "Yo, Bloom, Happy Bloomsday," waving their copies of *Ulysses*, from out of whose pages I'd stepped. —*Aaron Beall*

After having read so many sections at Bloomsday, and listened to more of them, it's not so much the Joycean games that dominate, but the reality of the novel. How vivid to me it is to walk into Bloom's bedroom, Molly there, warm in bed waiting for tea, the trip to the funeral, walking into that bar. The experience of Bloom has become part of my personal memory. —*David Margulies*

———

I've been doing Bloomsday at Symphony Space as long as they've been doing it. It's a delicious and bountiful day of literature. Isaiah [Sheffer] could be anyone from Molly to Leopold because he's such a great scholar and has assembled this event with great love. The Irish owe a great deal to the Jews. —*Malachy McCourt*

———

My favorite Joyce story was told to me by Gilbert Seldes many years ago. Many years before that, as a young, callow, and nervous reporter, he had managed to secure an interview with Joyce in Paris. All he could recall of the meeting, said Seldes, was that Joyce's favorite Irish whiskey was Jameson's. Because, said Joyce, according to Seldes, its distillery was downstream from a sewage outlet on the River Liffey—and thus contained the true essence of Dublin. Several grains of salt are recommended. —*Ray Gandolf*

———

I've taken part in Bloomsday at Symphony Space for all the years that it has been on. I missed it once (I was away doing a play), and on one occasion I made the stage with seconds to spare (had another performance). For me it's a great, joyous day. Isaiah [Sheffer] is an amazing performer, planner, organizer, director—I can't fathom how he does it. I've read the "Nausicaa" section for some years but recently off and on. I've read Molly Bloom's soliloquy. How lucky I am. I'm a Dubliner and have been a meanderer of Dublin streets like Mr. Joyce, in my time, so the book, the day, the celebration mean so much to me. I love the day. It's full of friends, words, joy, laughs! —*Terry Donnelly*

FIONNULA FLANAGAN ON BLOOMSDAY

Fionnula Flanagan, born and raised in Dublin, is among the foremost dramatic interpreters of James Joyce. Trained at Dublin's Abbey Theatre, Flanagan's portrayals of Gerty MacDowell, Molly Bloom, Sylvia Beach, Harriet Shaw Weaver, and Nora Joyce—in a variety of productions—have garnered her widespread critical acclaim and numerous awards, including Critics Circle Awards in Los Angeles and San Francisco, and a Tony Award nomination on Broadway. Today, Flanagan divides her time between homes in Ireland, Los Angeles, and Rancho Mirage, California, and continues to be a vital and familiar presence in American film and television.

Like James Joyce, I was born and raised in Dublin. Those years of the gray postwar fifties, seem to me now, looking back, to have been a time when Dublin was cobwebbed, as it were, by a leftover Edwardianism of a uniquely Irish kind. Many of the landmarks of Joyce's world remained, their coinage unchanged and in common usage—street names certainly, newspapers and adverts, shops and pubs, churches, restaurants and monuments, the turn of phrase, the prejudices, the mythologies, the past. My father, Terry, knew Dublin intimately, loved it fiercely. He would take us children on Sunday "rambles" into the inner-city during which odysseys he talked, nonstop, of its history. Bloom-like, we walked everywhere. On Saturday nights in my Grandma Flanagan's front parlor, while my aunts sipped port and conversed in whispers about "women's' ailments," my father and my uncles sang operatic arias loudly, drank whiskey, and hotly argued Irish politics. Shades of "The Dead" and "Ivy Day in the Committee Room," although I didn't yet know of the existence of those stories. Of course I also didn't know I was living in the geography of the very world Joyce had known and then recreated so brilliantly in his writings. Whenever my parents quoted or paraphrased him, casually—as in "Joyce understood that" or "As Joyce said..."—I just assumed he was someone they knew, an acquaintance from the vigorous Dublin intellectual set of their youth. But Joyce was everywhere in my childhood, in all the ordinary things we did that made up the fabric of our lives. We went to funerals in Glasnevin Cemetery—half my family is buried there—and on very special occasions we were treated to lunch at Jammets. We tramped out to the Shelley Banks and watched the Liverpool boat until it was just a speck, then raced miles out to find the tide on Sandymount Strand; we spied on the naked men swimming in the Forty Foot below the Martello Tower, where Buck Mulligan held his shaving bowl aloft. In summer the Howth tram swayed us to the top of the Head with its rhododendrons blazing purple and we tumbled on the grassy mound where Molly Bloom gazed out over Dublin Bay while Poldy pressed her to say "yes." I went to school in Eccles Street and walked by No. 7 twice a day. Of course the Blooms had lived there. Lived there still, had anyone asked me. For all that the house is gone, they are there yet.

My father participated actively in Dublin's first Bloomsday celebrations, welcoming Sylvia Beach, who graciously came from Paris to open the Martello Tower as a Joyce Museum.

My involvement as an actress in Joyce began with Joe Strick's film of *Ulysses* in which he cast me as Gerty MacDowell. Later on the great actor and director Burgess Meredith cast me to play Molly Bloom, and five other roles, opposite Zero Mostel in the 1974 Broadway revival of his production of *Ulysses in Nighttown*. That experience inspired me to go forward with developing and writing a theatrical tribute to the women who had been so central to Joyce's life and work. Called *James Joyce's Women*, it is a one-woman performance piece, which Burgess directed and in which I portrayed six women—three who sustained Joyce in his life and work (his wife, Nora Barnacle Joyce; and his two publishers, Sylvia Beach and Harriet Shaw Weaver), and three whom he immor-

talized through the miracle of his art (the Washerwoman from *Finnegans Wake*; and from *Ulysses* Gerty MacDowell and the timeless Molly Bloom). Thus began for me an invaluable mentoring relationship with Burgess Meredith and an award-winning stage production, which toured the United States, Australia, the Far East, and then Dublin as a highlight of the Joyce Centenary celebrations of 1982.

In 1985, Garrett O'Connor and I produced *James Joyce's Women* as a film, directed by Michael Pearce, which enjoyed considerable critical acclaim and continues to be favored by audiences worldwide on videotape.

Then along came Isaiah Sheffer, who loves Joyce and who invited me to read Molly's soliloquy one year at Bloomsday at Symphony Space in New York. I went onstage at ten p.m. and read nonstop for the following two hours and fifty minutes. It was both a terrifying and thrilling experience. I found in the swells and valleys of the soliloquy the sheer musical genius of Joyce, for it truly is a symphony in words. Over the years Isaiah has been kind enough to invite me back every second year to repeat the reading. It is one of the great pleasures of my life, and each time I learn more about Joyce, this extraordinary writer, creator of my childhood, fellow-countryman, fellow exile.

Boston/Martha's Vineyard, Massachusetts

Martha's Vineyard is now the home of the oldest continuous celebration of Bloomsday in the United States, which is sometimes even presented twice a year. John Crelan, the founder and director of Arts and Society and a motivated and creative Joyce devotee, started the festival in Boston in 1979, and eventually took it with him to Martha's Vineyard. Unlike many Bloomsday celebrations, it is not a time for reading aloud the text of *Ulysses*. The night is more of a performance than a recitation: It is a vehicle for original art within the spirit of Joyce, often a space for world premieres inspired by the text. The evening incorporates poems, lavish costume dramas, music, and dance—all based on Joyce's words—each year completely different from the last.

Arts and Society
P.O. Box 4485
Vineyard Haven, MA 02568

Tel: 508-696-0539
E-mail: jcrelan@yahoo.com
www.artsandsociety.org

Champaign-Urbana, Illinois

Founded by local musician Lisa Boucher, Bloomsday in Champaign-Urbana came into being through a diverse squadron of coconspirators, dancers, readers, singers, and frustrated former and current English majors. The group piles into Mike & Molly's, a local pub, to read selections aloud with frequent musical interludes. The event is a harmonic convergence between lovers of Irish music, of Joyce, and of Guinness. The Champaign Bloomsday celebration includes a James and Nora look-alike contest, Irish step-dancing, and Bloom's famous Gorgonzola lunch. Around two hundred people usually participate, either by reading selections, performing music, or lifting a pint or two in honor of Mr. Bloom.

A Joycean impression of the event by one participant:

'Tis everyone's favorite melody he hears:
—Would you like a Guinness?
—yes he said yes I will Yes.

P.O. Box 3201
Urbana, IL 61803
Tel: 217-359-0379
E-mail: lisa@fpmrecords.com
www.fpmrecords.com/events/bloomsday.html

Melbourne, Australia

Bloomsday in Melbourne aims to bring Joyce's novel alive for an ever-widening circle of readers, and by using an eclectic approach it has built a loyal and increasingly Joyce-literate community in Australia. A committee of writers produces original scripts that dramatize the novel in theatre, music, dance, film, multimedia, and art installations. One prominent theme is the connection of *Ulysses* and Dublin in the early twentieth century with the novel and Melbourne today. The entire city serves as a stage for Bloomsday performances and festivities. Bloomsday events are dispersed throughout the Melbourne historical neighborhoods that simultaneously evoke Joyce's Dublin while showing how this continent and era differ. Recent themes have included "Seawrack and Seaspawn," an exploration of Joyce's ideas on the cycles of decay, death, and renewal, along with a satiric critique of current Melbourne "urban renewal," and an examination of social change in gender relations since 1922. In 2002, there was a mock trial, in which a designated stand-in for Joyce withstood all sorts of intricate literary questions. Melbourne often commissions special works for the event: in 1999 a film "Australianising" the chapter "Lestrygonians"; also in 1999, a performance of the "Papal Bull Ballet" (culminating in the castration of the Papal Bull); and in 2000, an oratorio-style performance of *Finnegans Wake*. There have been Joycean party games during meals, speeches taken from the novel performed by well-known actors, mime shows, and even a slew of "Mollies" (male and female, Irish and Australian) cavorting over dinner.

Tel: 61-3-9372-9170
E-mail: dgill1999@hotmail.com
www.deakin.edu.au/arts/Bloomsite

A Bloomsday performer at Port Melbourne.

Philadelphia, Pennsylvania

The Rosenbach Museum and Library in Philadelphia is in possession of the original *Ulysses* manuscript, which contains more than eight hundred pages in Joyce's own handwriting. The year 2004 marks the Rosenbach's thirteenth annual Bloomsday Celebration, which will be longer and offer more public programs than on any previous June 16. In addition, the Rosenbach is inviting Joyce enthusiasts to join museum staff members on a trip to Dublin during the centenary celebration. The Bloomsday participants in this city actually wield the power to alter the urban landscape. Each year they close the 2000 block of DeLancey Place to traffic, and hundreds of chairs are set up for an all-day outdoor reading of *Ulysses*. Notable Philadelphians and Joyce fans come together and read the text to a large audience from the steps of the Rosenbach Museum.

Rosenbach Museum and Library
2008–2010 DeLancey Place
Philadelphia, PA 19103
Tel: 215-732-1600
E-mail: info@rosenbach.org
www.rosenbach.org

Sarasota, Florida

Beginning, as so many have, with a few volunteers and an extreme love of *Ulysses*, Bloomsday in Sarasota has grown tremendously since 2000. A biweekly group has emerged to discuss and celebrate Joyce throughout the entire year, and each annual Bloomsday celebration in Sarasota has had more than five hundred participants. It is now one of the largest literary events in southwest Florida. Visitors from around the state come to see films, hear Joyce-inspired music, see theatrical interpretations of his work, and participate in panel discussions. The group, now called the James Joyce Society of Sarasota, sponsored an academic conference to honor Joyce's 120th birthday in February 2002. Joyce scholars from throughout North America attended. In 2004, for the centennial celebration, "Jubilation Joyce!", organizers anticipate five days of Irish food and drink, dramatic readings by professional actors, original music composed especially for the occasion and performed on Sarasota's bayfront, scholarly lectures, films, performances, and new events that will mirror most of the eighteen chapters of *Ulysses* and involve the greater Sarasota community. In an effort to draw in a new generation of Joyceans, there will be an essay and creative writing contest in area high schools, and a "Youth Day" that will feature guest scholars, who will address teaching and writing about Joyce to pre-collegians, as well as a panel discussion among area teachers and students of Joyce.

The James Joyce Society of Sarasota, Inc.
P.O. Box 21298
Sarasota, FL 34276

Tel: 941-925-0453
E-mail: jsaunders@banshee.sar.usf.edu
www.bloomsdayinsarasota.org

San Diego, California

In the spirit of Bloomsday, many clubs choose to perform live reenactments of scenes from the novel, often with professional actors in period costume speaking lines from the text. A slightly different type of reenactment is performed on Bloomsday in San Diego. As *Ulysses* readers know, on June 16, 1904, Leopold Bloom took a tour of the pubs of Dublin. After stopping for lunch at a pub, Bloom went on to the Ormond Hotel for a pint and was tempted by the barmaids in the "Sirens" chapter. The San Diego Irish Players celebrate this portion of the novel by taking a double-decker bus to some of the best Irish pubs in San Diego and indulging in libations common to Joyce's period. On the bus ride, the Players read and listen to passages from *Ulysses* and other great Irish literature. The sponsor of the celebration, the "Ould Sod," strongly encourages costumes from the early 1900s. This tradition, called the "Literary Pub Crawl," is quite reminiscent of the original Bloomsday celebration held in Dublin in 1954.

The Ould Sod
3373 Adams Avenue
San Diego, CA 92116

Tel: 619-284-6594
E-mail: bloomsday@theouldsod.com
http://members.cox.net/gmelv/blooms.htm

Seattle, Washington

It seems that Joyce aficionados have a penchant for coming up with interesting names for themselves. Seattle is the home of the "Wild Geese Players," who have performed successive chapters of *Ulysses* every June 16 since 1998. Congressman Jim McDermott (Democrat of the Seventh District) is a participant, often playing the role of Bloom himself. With the support of the Seattle Irish Heritage Club, the actors lift the spirit of Joyce from the page and bring it to the stage in the roles of Leopold, Molly, Stephen, and others. The Wild Geese are aware that the very sounds of Joycean language are important in fully comprehending the book. In 2004, the Wild Geese Players plan to synchronize their performances with the time of day that the chosen scene appears in the novel. They take breaks only for cups of Irish coffee or a pint of the good stuff, and end their Bloomsday chapter readings with a curtain call. The cast (gradually joined by the audience) renders the Moore ballad "Just a Song at Twilight"!

Tel: 206-543-7155
E-mail: Bloomsday@irishclub.org
www.irishclub.org/ihcevents.htm

Syracuse, New York

The Syracuse James Joyce club was coincidentally founded on the fifty-third anniversary of James Joyce's death, on January 13, 1994. Dick Long was inspired to start the club after hosting a TV interview with a Joycean scholar who reminded him that he had never read the book. In order to escape "spending several years after death in a literary purgatory," Long decided to start a *Ulysses* reading group. Since 1994 the membership has grown tremendously in size and dedication, and it has created a tangible excitement about literature. Members write poetry about Joyce, compose songs for him, and are often inspired to honor him in original ways. The Syracuse James Joyce Club is one of the most active clubs around the world with about one hundred members meeting fortnightly in a different member's home. On Bloomsday, the performers read for thirteen hours in a local pub, the Bally Bay, with an average attendance during the day of about 350. Well-known readers in the past have included Julie Harris, while Seamus Heaney, a strong supporter, has been interviewed for the club newsletter. In addition to Bloomsday, each January, on the weekend of the anniversary of Joyce's death, Syracuse has a major reception to evoke his spirit, replete with tin whistle and pipe renditions, songs, witty offerings, and a variety of readings. A key element for Syracuse Bloomsday is the awarding of scholarships ($1000) to central New York college students and high school seniors who write winning essays or short stories with a theme relating to Joyce. The Scholarship Awards are intended to recognize the intellectual curiosity of young people and simultaneously promote the awareness in New York schools of Joyce's contribution to modern literature.

Tel: 315-622-1132
E-mail: bdillonm@arcomlabs.com
http://people.morrisville.edu/~loudismj/jjc

Toronto, Ontario

The Toronto Bloomsday festival begins with a question: "Why celebrate a man who never lived on a day that never existed?" and takes off from there. Toronto marks the anniversary with readings from *Ulysses* and Joyce's other works, and with music, song, and merriment, all of which were enormously important in Joyce's life. The festival has operated on these terms since 1986, and it has been manifested in a variety of different ways, from short readings on the beach in period wear to weeklong, full length, operatic-scale shows with actors, singers, and musicians. Besides love of Joyce, one of the reasons that people attend the Toronto Bloomsday festival is to savor Leopold Bloom's favorite dish at a local Irish pub. On June 16, 1904, Leopold Bloom stopped for a glass of Burgundy and a Gorgonzola sandwich at Davy Byrne's Pub, and may have created the most famous meal in literary history.

Anna Livia Productions
110 The Esplanade #103
Toronto, Ontario M5E 1X9

Tel: 416-365-7877
E-mail: livia@pathcom.com
www.pathcom.com/~livia

Bloomsday by Lake Ontario in Toronto.

James Joyce in Platzspitz, Zurich, 1937.

Ulysses in the Twenty-first Century

5

In an age when screen crawls and multitasking are the norm, the demands of Joyce's layered narrative and fractured consciousness hardly seem radical. And in an era in which images of explicit violence and sexuality are a mouse click away, relentlessly inviting us to view forbidden scenes, Joyce's obscenity seems tame. But *Ulysses* is still influential today, and remains a landmark of the literary landscape. How can one book be so enduring when most who have read it agree it was not an easy task?

Joyce's biographer Richard Ellmann argued that literature is by nature revolutionary, whether overtly or covertly. For Joyce this was especially true–this call to arms was at the moral center of his art. Joyce never proselytized the artistic and scientific methods central to modernism; his credo of silence, exile, and cunning didn't include such a public role as advocate. Instead he made his way through action, subverting the conventions of the novel. Joyce's role, in Ellmann's estimation, "was that of a sentry sounding an alarm, in the name of...a new humanity, active, unafraid and unashamed." In his essay entitled "The Consciousness of Joyce," Ellmann called *Ulysses* Joyce's Trojan horse: "a monument, but full of armed men; a comedy, but with teeth and claws."

Joyce used the techniques of the modernist experiment to create a single work that would take on the old guard. The soldiers of the Trojan horse have scattered, but their march is audible in the literature of the twenty-first century. In the last fifty years, realism has reasserted itself in English-language fiction, yet many authors— William Gaddis, Thomas Pynchon, and David Foster Wallace among them—have continued in the vein of the modernist experiment, using wordplay and double meanings, presenting interior monologues, rebelling against the authority of the central narrator, and replacing the hero with an antihero. Going back to Samuel Beckett, one finds echoes and parodies of Joyce; even Hemingway, an instant admirer of *Ulysses*, responded with direct language and short sentences, although perhaps more as a reaction to Henry James. On the other side are the proponents of the realist novel such as Philip Roth and John Updike. Even here, the reader finds evidence of the fractured perspective and elevation of the quotidian.

Thankfully, to borrow from Beckett, literary criticism is not bookkeeping, and the value of a work of art in any age is ultimately subjective. Joyce made *Ulysses* his manifesto on literature, but his message is never explicit, never concedes to the limitations of one meaning, one interpretation. *Ulysses* offers new meaning with each rereading. It offers challenge, mystery, sympathy, and humor. It is a treatise against complacency in writing, and a testament to the force of will Joyce mustered to soldier his own forces. And, using literary critic Malcolm Cowley's metaphor of a stone dropped into water, the arc of the ripples continues to widen.

The realm of *Ulysses'* influence extends beyond the front lines of the literary world. The year 2003 saw the publication of yet another Joyce biography, this time a book about his daughter, *Lucia Joyce: To Dance in the Wake*, by Carol Loeb Shloss. In addition to books on Joyce and his writing, *Ulysses* has inspired many creative works, among them the 1967 film *Ulysses*, a cinematic adaptation of Joyce's novel, directed by Joseph Strick and starring Milo O'Shea. Later came films of *A Portrait of the Artist as a Young Man* (1977); *The Dead* (1987), based on the *Dubliners* story; *James Joyce's Women* (1985), directed by Michael Pearce and starring Fionnula Flanagan, based on the writer's intimate relationships with the key women in his life; and more recently, *Nora* (2000), based on the Brenda Maddox biography of Nora Joyce and starring Ewan McGregor and Susan

Lynch. *Bl..m*, a *Ulysses* adaptation starring Stephen Rea, had its premiere in 2003.

In popular music, Kate Bush adapted lyrics from Molly's soliloquy for her song "The Sensual World" (1989), and Jefferson Airplane's "rejoyce" (1967) is inspired by Joyce's use of stream of consciousness, though it's doubtful Joyce anticipated his work colliding with sixties psychedelia. In 2003, the James Joyce Centre in Dublin produced a classical music compilation entitled *Classical Ulysses*. The protean nature of the *Ulysses*-effect is manifested in the cultures of high and low, as was the content of Joyce's novel

In the twenty-first century, *Ulysses* has many roles to play. In addition to inspiring new works of literature and art, and being the focus of annual worldwide celebrations, *Ulysses* has shaped our culture in other ways less obvious but worthy of note. The issue of censorship is integral to the genesis of *Ulysses* and it extends into the areas of copyright and ownership of the novel, as well as other works of art, today. As a cultural artifact with the accompanying responsibilities of preservation and scholarship, *Ulysses* is prized. In the literary world, translators continually confront the challenges of *Ulysses*, and with each new translation, the international circle of readership widens. Lastly, as a contribution to the literary canon, in the classrooms of universities around the world, Joyce's legacy is very much alive today.

One way in which *Ulysses* will continue to reverberate in the current century—appropriately, given the specifics of *Ulysses*' unique publication history—has to do with its copyright status. A source of contention since the book's publication in 1922, there is to this day disagreement about exactly when the copyrights of *Ulysses* expire in which territories of the world. Additionally, the publication of Joyce's private papers and those of his family has been severely restricted (in some cases, letters have allegedly been destroyed)—which, while protecting the family's privacy, inevitably has had a dampening effect on would-be creative adaptations of the book as well as on scholarly inquiries into it.

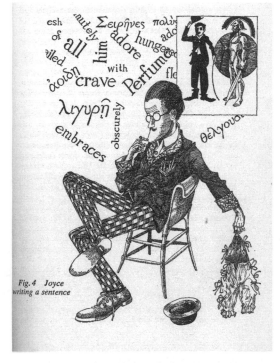

"Joyce Writing a Sentence," drawing by Guy Davenport.

ULYSSES, BLOOMSDAY, AND COPYRIGHT
Robert Spoo

Robert Spoo, a Joyce scholar and former editor of the James Joyce Quarterly, *was inspired by the complexities of both the novel and legal ambiguities surrounding* Ulysses *to become an intellectual property attorney. He reflects on the purpose of copyright, the status of* Ulysses, *and what its future is likely to hold.*

Copyrights are blessedly porous things; they let spill into the public domain almost as much as they withhold from it. It may come as a surprise that many intellectual property lawyers are as emphatic about the limitations of copyright law as they are about the private entitlements it confers. These lawyers know that copyright law, in the United States anyway, is at bottom a pragmatic inducement to creation, a kind of statutory bait and switch aimed at tempting authors out of silence and inactivity and into expression. In exchange for expressing their ideas in tangible forms, authors are given a strictly temporary monopoly, at the end of which the work is taken from the copyright owner and handed over bodily to the public. Even during its statutory term of protection there are many things that a copyright cannot control: fair-use quotation, parody, loose paraphrase, copying of general plot elements and themes, character types, ideas, and literary styles. Many of the spontaneous emulations that take place every Bloomsday are classic examples of this other side of copyright.

Once a copyright has played its part in inducing creation and compensating the creator, and after a specified term of years, the work is turned over to the management of the public domain, where, in contrast to the limited perspectives and goals of a sole copyright owner, countless users are free to exercise their ingenuity in ferreting out the work's hidden potential in the form of adaptations, performances, and other transformative uses. That the work will be exposed to irreverent treatment is no argument against the ending of its copyright. One test of a masterpiece is its resilience despite subjection to parody, bawdry, and cultural vandalism. The mustache on the Mona Lisa always washes off.

The benefits of the public domain to society as a whole are significant and demonstrable: Think of Leonard Bernstein's modernization of *Romeo and*

Juliet in *West Side Story*; Jean Rhys's recasting of *Jane Eyre* in *Wide Sargasso Sea*; and all those classic Disney features that clothe traditional tales in rich colors and fetching animation. None of these works could have been produced for public consumption—without elaborate and possibly paralyzing negotiations—had their authors not been free to draw on works that had become a part of the shared cultural treasury. *Ulysses* itself, with its wealth of quotation, allusion, and literary imitation, would scarcely be the work it is had Joyce been required to negotiate licenses with the estates of Homer and Shakespeare and all the other authors woven into the tapestry of Bloomsday. The public domain means never having to say please.

Yet, because of the increasing length and scope of present-day copyrights, our relationship to *Ulysses* is quite different from Joyce's relationship to the works of his own literary heritage. Copyright plays a large, sometimes daunting role in our experience of *Ulysses*, and this role will continue well into the twenty-first century in many parts of the world. In the United Kingdom and the Republic of Ireland, for example, *Ulysses* will remain in copyright until the end of 2011. Nearly a century of legal protection can scarcely be justified on any theory consistent with copyright's core pragmatic purpose of adding a dash of economic incentive to the other attractions of authorship. Overlong copyright terms inspire misconceptions about the nature of intellectual property, causing copyright owners and the public alike to think of copyrights as family heirlooms or corporate entitlements. But grandmother's brooch was never intended to play the important social and cultural role for which a creative work like *Ulysses* is destined. Fame overtook Joyce's novel almost before it was published in book form, and every year that passes witnesses more intense popular interest in the work, almost as if its reputation for hermetic intellectualism only made the world more eager to unlock its essential human simplicity.

The Joyce copyrights have encouraged their share of creative suppressions. Recently, Cork University Press published a large, handsome anthology of twentieth-century Irish writing, the comprehensiveness of which would have been total had the Press not been required at the last minute to excise—literally—the section devoted to Joyce extracts. In place of the shorn pages the Press inserted a cardboard blank bearing the notice, "Pages 323–346 have been removed due to a dispute in relation to copyright." Around the same time, a young Irish composer was denied permission to use eighteen words from *Finnegans Wake* in a short choral piece he had written on commission for a Europe-wide radio broadcast. More even than losing the commission and the broadcast, the composer regretted that "my piece can't ever exist because it can't be performed." Public-spirited as they are in theory, copyrights have their ruthless aspect as well.

However one feels about the proper role of copyright, and whatever the disagreement surrounding the status of *Ulysses,* it is important to bear in mind that in the not-too-distant future, *Ulysses* will ineluctably join the cultural commons (barring further legislative extensions of copyright). It is a pleasurable exercise to consider what the results might be. Surely we will see new and imaginative editions of *Ulysses,* both in print and in e-book formats; electronic multimedia presentations of the novel, perhaps with hotlinks to Joyce criticism and manuscript materials and interactive Dublin maps, music, and vintage photographs; Internet Bloomsday readings of the whole book, organized on an international basis; and countless cinematic and theatrical adaptations of the wanderings of the latter-day Odysseus and Telemachus. One or another of these adaptations might even speculate intrepidly on whether Molly really does give Leopold another chance, come the morning of June 17.

On that red-letter day for the public domain, *Ulysses* will finally take its place with *The Odyssey* and *The Divine Comedy* as raw mythmaking material for some future national epic. Indeed, it could be argued that a work does not really become a "classic" until it is unqualifiedly available for cultural exploitation. It would follow that overlong copyrights are an inhibition on the full organic development and destiny of classic works.

Undoubtedly, a public-domain *Ulysses* will spur countless acts of creativity and scholarship and add greatly to the cultural wealth of the United States and the world. Not insignificantly, it will make Bloomsday an even more joyous event than it already is. Both the day and the book that created it will then enter fully into the democracy of public uses. And one very long copyright will at last be at an end.

Ulysses is more than intellectual property, or for that matter, an object for artistic consumption; it exists as a physical and cultural artifact with all the attributes that artifacts carry.

The first edition of *Ulysses*, published by Sylvia Beach's Shakespeare and Company, was a limited edition of 1,000. Of those, 750 copies were printed on handmade paper, and Joyce signed 100 copies. These copies sell for up to $100,000 today.

Ulysses manuscripts have become even more valuable. "*Ulysses*, like everything else of Joyce's, was written entirely by hand," Beach recalled. "He used blunt black pencils—he found the ones he wanted at Smith's in Paris—and pencils of different colors to distinguish the parts he was working on." An autographed manuscript of a previously unknown draft of the "Circe" chapter in *Ulysses* was sold at a Christie's auction in 2000 for $1.4 million to the National Library of Ireland in Dublin. Scholars and curators have worked to preserve these documents and make the drafts available for public view, revealing more intimate aspects of Joyce's creative process.

A HANDWRITTEN ODYSSEY: JOYCE'S MANUSCRIPTS
Mike Barsanti

The Rosenbach Museum and Library in Philadelphia owns one of the few complete manuscripts of Ulysses. *Visitors can look at the pages, written in Joyce's hand, complete with revisions and notes. Mike Barsanti, the associate director of the museum, discusses the evolution and legacy of Joyce's working method.*

James Joyce quickly learned that his scrawled drafts were worth money to collectors. In the spring of 1917, the New York lawyer, collector, and patron John Quinn purchased several manuscripts from him, including the manuscript of his play *Exiles*. This transaction, arranged by Ezra Pound, made a deep impression. A year later Joyce told Pound that he intended to sell the manuscript of *Ulysses* in order to pay for the typing.

Joyce agreed to sell the manuscript to Quinn in 1920, two years before the book was finished. For Quinn, the purchase was a way of subsidizing a worthy writer. Joyce would send episodes to Quinn more or less as he finished them, and Quinn would send money back. In 1923 Quinn decided to sell most of his books and manuscripts at auction. The Ulysses manuscript was purchased for $1,975 by Dr. A. S. W. Rosenbach, one of the greatest book dealers of his time. Joyce was bitterly disappointed by the low price, even more so when he learned that Rosenbach had bought a group of Joseph Conrad manuscripts at the same auction—one of them for more than $8,000. Joyce looked into buying the manuscript back, but decided against it. Rosenbach never offered the *Ulysses* manuscript for sale. It became part of his personal collection, and is now part of the collection of the museum he founded with his brother Philip—the Rosenbach Museum and Library in Philadelphia.

The Rosenbach Manuscript is the only complete, handwritten draft of *Ulysses*. It is sometimes described as a "fair copy," meaning that it is a fairly clean, readable version copied from earlier, messier drafts and made to be read by a typist. A few chapters appear to have been written out hastily so that Joyce could send them to Quinn for some quick cash. Still, it shows many signs of Joyce's characteristic habit of adding new material at every possible opportunity. The many changes made to the text in progress, combined with Joyce's weak eyesight and the circumstance of the book being typeset by French printers led to an extraordinary number of errors in the first edition. No edition published since has been free of them.

Word play, the high and the low, the antihero: these concerns were central to modernist literature. But additionally, Joyce's novel explores the conscious and subconscious mind. The depiction of these states of mind provides a challenge for the translator who strives to make *Ulysses* available in foreign words while remaining faithful not only to language but also to the ideas.

Ellmann noted Joyce's enjoyment of language play. "The pun," he wrote, "pervades Joyce's work as if it were a way in which the artist could imitate the duplexity of nature....The pun, verbal emblem of coincidence, agent of democracy and collectivist ideas, makes all the quirky particles of the world stick to each other by hook or by crook. Such adhesiveness is unity or the closest to unity that can be envisaged."

Nothing is more emblematic of the ever-widening impact of Joyce's novel than its translation and dissemination into many languages. Since it was published (legally) in the United States in 1934, other countries have followed suit, and now we can count more than forty translations of *Ulysses*, among them Arabic, Catalan, Czech, Croatian, Danish, Dutch, Finnish, French, Gaelic, German, Hungarian, Icelandic, Italian, Japanese, Malayalam, Norwegian, Polish, Portuguese, Slovenian, Spanish, Swedish, and Turkish.

In articulating the challenges of translating *Ulysses* into Chinese, the scholar Jin Di delivers some illuminating recollections, and his commitment to the intricacies of Joyce's language offers further insight into the book. Born in China, Jin has worked as a translator since his undergraduate studies in English literature in the early 1940s. He spent a decade as a fellow at the University of Virginia and the National Humanities Center, where he completed his Chinese translation of *Ulysses*.

With regard to the difficulties of this endeavor he explains, "In the case of a translator working in a language as distant as Chinese, understandably his difficulty is more than doubled. Not to mention the special syntactic and stylistic features which are Joycean wonders in English but which sometimes are nightmares to the poor translator, even the rendering of the simplest of words can cause headaches unknown to his colleagues working in European languages."

YES I SAID: TRANSLATING *ULYSSES* INTO CHINESE
by Jin Di

Any reader of Molly Bloom's soliloquy knows the rapturous effect of yes *when repeated breathlessly by Molly in English. However, it poses particular challenges to the translator. Following are excerpts from an interview with Simon Loekle that appeared in* Poets and Writers *magazine in November/December 2002.*

Joyce's deliberately repeated use of *yes*, as what he called "the woman word," in the final episode to characterize Molly's mentality is at odds with the genius of the Chinese language, which requires lexical adjustments to express the multitude of ideas carried by the English *yes*. There is not one Chinese term, much less the standard "counterpart"—*shi-de*—that can in a Chinese version of the novel more or less consistently replace *yes*. This contrasts with such European language counterparts as *si*, *oui*, *ja*, and so on, in their versions. If I followed Joyce's lead and repeated one Chinese term in all the eighty-odd occasions in the chapter where *yes* is found in the original, I would most certainly ruin the end text with expressions that would sound idiotic to most Chinese readers. Joyce's demand for emphatic repetition runs head-on into a conflict with the genius of the Chinese language.

After a long and careful study I decided that a large number of Molly's *yes*es do not serve as much more than a kind of emphatic affirmation of the speaker's own sincerity. There is hardly any other substantive content to those *yes*es, so it is possible to choose a Chinese term of affirmation that sounds natural on such occasions. This decision meant fewer repetitions of Joyce's *yes*, but enough to produce an impression of a habitual locution in someone's mouth, as "the woman word" must do.

The repeatable term of emphatic affirmation I chose is *zhen-de*— "really"—which is a kind of habitual locution with some speakers of Chinese. It is repeated dozens of times in my translation of the last episode, and like Joyce's *yes*, it does stand both at the beginning and the end of it, conspicuously but quite naturally. At the same time, the other *yes*es are rendered flexibly, each in a way that suits its particular context. Some of the *yes*es in the final passage of the episode, for instance, involve the very serious matter of accepting a marriage proposal, for which neither *shi-de* nor *zhen-de* will suffice.

My rendering for that is *yuan-yi*, a formal term that means "I will."

Yet in its Chinese form the pronoun *I* is understood, and the ending of the novel becomes "yuan-yi wo yuan-yi zhen-de." I believe this carries the same emphasis as Joyce's original *yes I will Yes.*—which in fact happens to be its only back-translation.

Joyce believed his purpose to be exalted: in art, his aim was life; in life, his aim was art. He fought untiringly in the face of monumental opposition. His confidence was gargantuan, as was his intellectual appetite. In *Ulysses* he set his sights on the history of the Western language and literature, from Homer to the contemporary Irish poets, but the scope of his vision was never limited to literature. His method of composition was modeled on the paradoxical nature of life; the conflict of vice and virtue, depicting these opposing forces with what Beckett termed "aesthetic vigilance." As subject matter, Joyce chose politics, aesthetics, and the morality of art. His writing addressed the complexities of human experience and perception, mimicking the fractured nature of human consciousness. As Beckett said, Joyce's writing wasn't about something, "it was the thing itself."

As students around the world read *Ulysses*, together with fellow students and accompanied by the insight of their professors, the experience is unique for each individual. Time alters the impressions that any work of art effects, and what registered as shocking nearly a century ago no longer shocks. What is not diminished is the universal in Joyce's novel, that which is recognized by all who have read it; it is the evidence of one who fought untiringly against mortality, and the clarity of that mission. This is the legacy that remains unaltered by time, into the twenty-first century, and for as long as *Ulysses* is read.

ULYSSES WITHOUT TEARS:
TEACHING THE YOUNG A DIFFICULT BOOK
Mary Gordon

In the halls and rooms where young minds are shaped, Joyce's legacy carries perhaps the most weight. The novelist, essayist, and professor Mary Gordon speaks to the unending influence of Ulysses.

Each academic year, I teach *Ulysses* to undergraduates. Let us both bear in mind that these are undergraduates at a prestigious Ivy League institution (Barnard College of Columbia University) and so the group of which we are speaking is representative, perhaps, only of itself. But however distinguished they are, my students are young and members of a generation famous for its ahistoricity, its short attention span. You know: The MTV generation who could use computers before they could walk, think that *gangsta* is a perfectly acceptable adjective, know the ins and outs of textmessaging but never heard of litotes or metonymy. What, you may ask, does *Ulysses* have to say to them? And, you may be tempted to ask, more urgently: What do I have to say to them about *Ulysses*?

I begin by assuring them that they are not alone in thinking that *Ulysses* is difficult. And that, in fact, Joyce wants it to be difficult. Why, they ask me, would someone want to make things difficult? I tell them that it has to be difficult because Joyce wanted to include so much of the civilized world, so much that it requires years of learning to gain access to. And then I try to be honest with them about Joyce the bully. "Imagine you had a friend," I tell them, "who is a bully. An intellectual bully. He really enjoys knowing that he's read much more than you. He often throws out references that you can't possibly get, and when you can't get them, you notice a little smirk of satisfaction (is it self-satisfaction?) at the corner of his lips. Why do you put up with him? Why do you continue to spend time with him? Because he tells great jokes and knows the words to absolutely wonderful songs. And he has a friend whom he travels with who's a lot nicer than he is."

The music and the jokes: This is the way I bring students to *Ulysses*. I forbid them to read Stuart Gilbert, the eminent Joyce scholar. I tell them to forget, at first, finding Homeric parallels. I always teach the book in the springtime; often I am lucky: The weather is on my side. After they've read the first chapter, I tell them to choose a partner. I send them outdoors for fifteen minutes. I have them read aloud to one another. Then we come back. Every time, they are relieved of their anxiety; they have lost themselves in the music. We look at all the different kinds of music in the first chapters: from the sacred *In Paradisum* to the profane "Ballad of Joking Jesus." Then we go for the jokes.

The two chapters of *Ulysses* that are best for jokes are the "Cyclops" and "Nausicaa." The nationalism that shapes "Cyclops" begins in comedy and ends in violence; its fossil fuel is alcohol. I ask them to enjoy the fun of the many words and phrases these professional drinkers employ when urging each on for another pint. We revel in the absurdity of the narrator's attributing Irishness to almost everyone of note who ever drew breath. The "Irish heroes and heroines of antiquity" include the Village Blacksmith, Dante Alighieri, Christopher Columbus, Charlemagne, the Mother of the Maccabees, the last of the Mohicans, Benjamin Franklin, Napoleon Bonaparte, Cleopatra, Patrick W. Shakespeare, Lady Godiva, and the Queen of Sheba. I tell them the story of a friend of mine who insists that everyone worthwhile is Jewish, including El Greco and, of course, Shakespeare. In our murderous times, the violence always under the surface of nationalism is a topic not difficult for them to relate to, nor is the always accessible strain of anti-Semitism that inflames the citizen when Bloom reminds the crowd that Jesus was a Jew.

When we turn to the "Nausicaa" chapter, I tell them to try to imagine this hyperintellectual fellow, self-exiled from his native Dublin, sitting in Italy writing to his aunt in Dublin for the latest in women's trash magazines. The over-the-top language Gerty invokes when she fantasizes about Bloom has not changed for the writers of today's Harlequin romances: "She could see at once by his pale intellectual face that he was a foreigner." Gerty's self-deception, her inability to acknowledge her own dark sexual side, is the stuff of advice columnists of 2004; Gerty's rules and rituals are no different from Charlotte's in *Sex and the City*. I ask them if the products that Gerty MacDowell thinks of using are different from the products they might read about in, if not *Harper's Bazaar* or *Vogue*, then one of the less upmarket women's mags on the racks near the supermarket checkout. (This is easy because most of my students are women.) I ask them to think, in the recesses of their hearts, of the last foolish cosmetic purchase they made.

Then we turn to Gerty:

> Why have women such eyes of witchery? Gerty's were of the bluest
> Irish blue, set off by lustrous lashes and dark expressive brows. Time
> was when those brows were not so silkyseductive. It was Madame
> Vera Verity, directress of the Woman Beautiful page of the Princess
> novelette, who had first advised her to try eyebrowleine Which gave
> that haunting expression to the eyes, so becoming in leaders of fash-
> ion, and she had never regretted it. Then there was blushing scientifi-
> cally cured and how to be tall increase your height and you have a
> beautiful face but your nose?

We all have fun with Gerty's cheap feminine claptrap, and then we watch
Bloom watching her, and we all enjoy the fireworks. And then, the let-
down—Gerty is not whole; Gerty is disabled—and we sink into the swamp
of Bloom's unattractive postcoital sludge: It was all her fault. The woman
tempted me and I did eat.

I point out to them that at the very time that Bloom was looking at the white
circle of Gerty's crotch, the chapter travels to the men in the church, at the
ceremony of benediction. They are watching the white circle of the host,
adoring in their way as Bloom does in his. And I remind them (there are
some benefits to having a teacher who grew up in Irish Catholicism) that
the short prayers offered at Benediction are referred to as Ejaculations. I
ask them to enjoy the weaving of the sacred and profane, the ancient beau-
ties and the detritus of the commercial, which are the warp and woof of
Joyce's enterprise.

And as city dwellers, they live in a world that allows them to revel in the
delights of both high and low. Bloom is an ad-man and their lives are inun-
dated with advertising; rather than excoriating this tendency, Joyce has
fun with it. "What is home without Plumtree's potted meat? Incomplete?"
The poignancy of the book is in Bloom's mock heroism; this kind man
reaching, unsuccessfully, for something greater, of which he has an
inchoate hint, the partially faithful husband of a flagrantly unfaithful but
finally faithful wife—all set against the implacable idealism of Stephen's

literary pursuits and moral scrupulosities. This mixture of *Ulysses* is the mix that makes up their lives.

Only after they've had fun with *Ulysses* and learned to love it, I tell them, is it time to look at the Homeric parallels. This is not a book, I tell them, that you read once only. I know that at least some of them have gone back to it. I call this a success.

Biographical Notes

NORA BARNACLE (1884–1951): Joyce's wife, born in Galway, Ireland. Nora worked as a chambermaid at Finn's Hotel, Dublin, when Joyce met her. The couple eloped in 1904 and were legally married on July 4, 1931.

DJUNA BARNES (1892–1982): American novelist, short story writer, playwright, and illustrator.

SYLVIA BEACH (1887–1962): American-born Paris bookseller. Became the first publisher of *Ulysses* in 1922; the novel was released under the imprint of her bookstore, Shakespeare and Company.

SAMUEL BECKETT (1906–1989): Poet, novelist, dramatist, short story writer, and translator. Born in Foxrock, County Dublin. Studied at Trinity College, Dublin. Settled in Paris in 1937 where he lived most of his adult life. Received Nobel Prize for Literature in 1969.

FRANCIS BLAKE (dates unknown): Library Attendant at the National Library of Ireland, where he became acquainted with Joyce.

FRANK BUDGEN (1882–1971): Friend of Joyce's, author of *James Joyce and the Making of Ulysses* (1934). Born in England, he eventually settled in Paris to study painting. Moved to Zurich during World War I, met Joyce in 1918.

DR. JOSEPH COLLINS (dates unknown): Reviewed *Ulysses* in *The New York Times*, 1922.

MALCOLM COWLEY (1898–1989): American critic and poet.

HART CRANE (1899–1932): American poet.

Constantine Curran (1880–1972): A lifelong friend of Joyce's after they met at University College, Dublin.

James Douglas (dates unknown): Reviewed *Ulysses* in the *Dublin Sunday Express*, 1922.

T. S. Eliot (1888–1965): American-born English poet, playwright, and publisher.

Richard Ellmann (1918–1987): American biographer, scholar, and editor. His definitive biography, *James Joyce*, first published in 1959, is a singular contribution to Joyce studies. His other subjects included William Butler Yeats and Oscar Wilde.

Morris L. Ernst (1888–1976): Counsel for Random House in its case for publication of *Ulysses* in the United States.

William Faulkner (1897–1962): American novelist. Received Nobel Prize in Literature in 1949.

Emeric Fischer (dates unknown): Reviewed *Ulysses* in the French journal *Revue Française*.

F. Scott Fitzgerald (1896–1940): American novelist and short story writer.

Ford Madox Ford (1873–1939): English novelist, critic, and editor.

Roger Fry (1866–1934): English art critic and painter, and member of the Bloomsbury group, a circle of writers and artists in London.

Stuart Gilbert (1883–1969): British critic, translator, and close friend of Joyce. Wrote *James Joyce's Ulysses* (1930), an early book-length study of the novel, when the novel was still hard to obtain.

LOUIS GILLET (1876–1943): Literary critic who wrote a negative review of Joyce. He later revoked it, and he and Joyce became friends.

OLIVER ST. JOHN GOGARTY (1878–1957): Irish physician, poet, playwright, novelist, essayist, and member of the Irish senate. The *Ulysses* character Buck Mulligan is based on Gogarty. Joyce and Gogarty met in 1902 at the National Library of Ireland, became friends, and in 1904 Joyce stayed with Gogarty at the Martello Tower in Sandycove. After Joyce lampooned Gogarty in the poem "Holy Office" their friendship ended, although Gogarty made attempts to reconcile later, to no avail. Gogarty was the model for several characters in Joyce's fiction.

HERBERT GORMAN (1893–1954): American newspaper reporter, critic, and writer. Author of *James Joyce: His First Forty Years* (1924).

ERNEST HEMINGWAY (1899–1961): American writer of novels and short stories. Received Nobel Prize in Literature in 1954.

SISLEY HUDDLESTON (1883–1952): English writer and journalist, lived in Paris. Posted to Paris during World War I, Huddleston became an expert in French politics and history. He socialized with and wrote about the literary and artistic expatriates of Paris. He was so often to be found at Sylvia Beach's English-language bookshop Shakespeare and Company that he was dubbed "Mr. Shakespeare."

CHRISTOPHER ISHERWOOD (1904–1986): Writer of fiction, biography, and plays in collaboration with W. H. Auden. Born in Cheshire, England, lived in Berlin, became a U.S. citizen in 1946.

MARIA JOLAS (1893–1987): Born in Louisville, Kentucky, the great-grandniece of Thomas Jefferson; she moved to Paris in 1925 with her husband, Eugene Jolas. Jolas and Elliot Paul founded *Translation*, a literary magazine that printed episodes of *Finnegans Wake*.

LUCIA JOYCE (1907–1982): Second child of James and Nora, born in Trieste. While living in Paris in the 1920s she pursued a career in dance with some success. By 1929 Lucia showed signs of severe mental distress, which eventually led to her institutionalization. In 1934 C. G. Jung agreed to work with her, to no avail. After World War II, Lucia was moved to St. Andrew's hospital in Northampton, England, where she remained until her death.

STANISLAUS JOYCE (1884–1955): James's younger brother. He was his brother's confidant and later provided much-needed financial support. When James left for Paris in 1920, Stanislaus remained in Trieste and their relationship cooled. In 1928 he married, and when he died he left behind a wife, Nelly, and a son, James, born in 1943.

CARL GUSTAV JUNG (1875–1961): Swiss analytical psychologist. Broke with Sigmund Freud and eventually founded his own school of analytical psychology in Zurich.

FRANK KERMODE (b. 1919): English critic, cultural historian, and English Renaissance scholar.

PAUL L. LÉON (1893–1942): Close friend to Joyce and family for the last decade the Joyces lived in Paris. Emigrated from Russia in 1918. Léon assisted Joyce from 1930 to 1940 as a consultant and intermediary in various professional capacities. After the Joyces left Paris in 1940, Léon, a Jew, put himself at personal risk to retrieve Joyce's papers from the Joyces' Paris apartment. He deposited the collection at the National Library of Ireland, where it remained sealed for fifty years. Léon was arrested by the Gestapo in Paris in 1941 and died in a concentration camp.

WYNDHAM LEWIS (1882–1957): Canadian-born British artist, critic, satirist, and novelist. Proponent of Vorticism, a literary and artistic movement in England dedicated to abstraction, that lasted through the early 1900s.

JAMES CLARENCE MANGAN (1803–1849): Irish poet whose work Joyce championed as a young man. Early on, Joyce saw Mangan as an artist whose talents received little or no recognition and whose life ended in despair, and later as an example of the dangers of an art that relies on romanticism and sentimental nationalism.

ROBERT MCALMON (1896–1956): American poet, short story writer, and publisher who lived in Paris between the world wars and became friends with Joyce in Paris.

HENRY MILLER (1891–1980): American writer who lived in Paris.

ADRIENNE MONNIER (1892–1955): Close friend and supporter of Joyce, and companion of Sylvia Beach. Owned a bookshop, the Maison des Amis des Livres, on rue de l'Odéon, across the street from Beach's Shakespeare and Company. Influential in the French literary scene between World War I and II.

VLADIMIR NABOKOV (1899–1977): Novelist, taught language and grammar in the Russian Department at Wellesley College and Slavic Literature at Cornell University. Born in St. Petersburg, Russia, studied at Cambridge; became a U.S. citizen in 1945.

CARDINAL JOHN HENRY NEWMAN (1801–1890): Anglican cleric, instrumental in the Anglo-Catholic Oxford Movement. Converted in 1845 and eventually became a cardinal in the Roman Catholic Church. In 1854 Newman became the first rector of the Catholic University of Dublin, forerunner of University College, Dublin.

ALFRED NOYES (1880–1958): English poet.

EDNA O'BRIEN (b. 1932): Irish novelist, short story writer, and playwright. Author of a biography of Joyce.

EZRA POUND (1885–1972): American poet, translator, and critic.

ARTHUR POWER (1891–1984): Irish writer, friend of Joyce.

JOHN QUINN (1870–1924): American attorney, arts patron, and manuscripts collector.

DR. A. S. W. ROSENBACH (1876–1952): Dealer in rare books and manuscripts with his brother and business partner, Philip Rosenbach (1863–1953), a dealer in fine art and antiques. The Rosenbach Company, with offices in Philadelphia and New York City, was recognized as a leading trader in rare books and manuscripts.

SAMUEL ROTH (1894–1974): Austrian-born American poet, editor, and avant-garde publisher. In July 1926, Roth began printing portions of *Ulysses* in a journal, *Two Worlds Monthly*, without Joyce's permission. In December 1928 the New York courts secured an order, under the initiative of Joyce's American lawyer, enjoining further publication.

GEORGE BERNARD SHAW (1856–1950): Irish dramatist, critic, and social reformer. Member of the Fabian Society, a socialist political organization in Great Britain.

PHILIPPE SOUPAULT (1897–1990): French poet, novelist, and critic. Founder of Surrealism with André Breton.

STEPHEN SPENDER (1909–1995): English poet and critic.

GERTRUDE STEIN (1874–1946): American poet, novelist, and critic.

Prominent expatriate in Paris. Raised in Philadelphia, settled in Paris in 1903.

HARRIET SHAW WEAVER (1876–1961): Longtime patron and close friend of Joyce and his family. Born in Cheshire, became an ardent feminist, and in 1936 joined the Communist Party. Editor at *The Egoist*, and later served as a literary critic, personal confidante, and financial adviser to Joyce. Weaver's financial support enabled Joyce to devote his working time to writing.

EDITH NEWBOLD WHARTON (1862–1937): American novelist and short story writer. Born in New York, settled in Paris in 1907 with her husband, Edward Wharton.

TENNESSEE WILLIAMS (1911–1983): American playwright, fiction writer, poet, and essayist.

WILLIAM CARLOS WILLIAMS (1883–1963): American poet, novelist, and a practicing physician.

EDMUND WILSON (1895–1972): American literary critic, social commentator, and novelist. His essay on Joyce was one of the first serious American literary assessments of *Ulysses*.

VIRGINIA WOOLF (1882–1941): English novelist, critic, and essayist.

JOHN WOOLSEY (1877–1945): U.S. District Court judge in landmark case paving way for publication of *Ulysses* in the United States.

WILLIAM BUTLER YEATS (1865–1939): Irish poet and dramatist. Son of Irish painter John Butler Yeats.

Contributors

MICHAEL BARSANTI is Associate Director of the Rosenbach Museum and Library in Philadelphia.

JIN DI was born in China and has worked as a translator since his years as a student of English literature in the early 1940s. He has been a Visiting Fellow at the Simpson Center, University of Washington. Jin's Chinese translation of Joyce's *Ulysses* is recognized as a monumental achievement and a work of art. In addition to translations of *Ulysses*, he has written widely on the theoretical and practical aspects of translation, most recently *Literary Transliteration: Quest for Artistic Integrity*.

FIONNULA FLANAGAN is a distinguished stage and screen actress whose recent credits include *The Others, Divine Secrets of the Ya-Ya Sisterhood, Some Mother's Son, Waking Ned Devine,* and the forthcoming films *Sexual Life* and *Samantha's Child*. She is married to Garrett O'Connor, a physician, and divides her time between her homes in Ireland, Los Angeles, and Rancho Mirage, California.

MARY GORDON is professor of English at Barnard College, professor of writing at Columbia, and the best-selling author of five novels, a book of novellas, a collection of short stories, three collections of essays, a nonfiction book on Joan of Arc, and a memoir. She is the recipient of the Lila Acheson Wallace Reader's Digest Award, a Guggenheim Fellowship, and the 1997 O. Henry Prize for best short story.

FRANK MCCOURT was born in New York and raised in Limerick, Ireland. At the age of nineteen, McCourt returned to the United States and embarked on a career as a New York City public high school teacher. His memoir *Angela's Ashes* won a Pulitzer Prize and went on to win the National Book Critics Circle Award and the *Los Angeles Times* Book Award.

ISAIAH SHEFFER is a playwright and lyricist who is also the co-founder and the Artistic Director of Symphony Space, one of the leading performance venues in New York City. He is the co-creator, host, director, and a favorite performer of "Bloomsday on Broadway," a New York institution for twenty-three years. He is also host and director of the "Selected Shorts" series, which pairs Oscar and Tony Award-winning actors with short stories by acclaimed contemporary and classic authors.

ROBERT SPOO is an intellectual property attorney, a scholar of copyright law in its connections with modern literature and poetry, and former editor of the *James Joyce Quarterly* and professor of English at the University of Tulsa.

LETTIE TEAGUE is the wine editor and a columnist for *Food & Wine* magazine and recipient of the 2003 James Beard M.F.K. Fisher Award for Distinguished Writing.

NOLA TULLY is an editor and writer. Her art and photography reviews have appeared in *DoubleTake*, *Nerve*, and *AfterImage*; her fiction has appeared in *Ploughshares*; and she has taught writing at Columbia and New York Universities. She has worked at several magazines, including *Entertainment Weekly*, *Audubon*, and *Civilization*, both in freelance and staff positions, and in the publications department at the International Center of Photography. From 1989 to 1991 she worked as a photojournalist with Sygma Photo News (now Corbis Sygma), and her photographs have appeared in *Time*, *Life*, *Newsweek*, *Paris Match*, *New York*, and many other news magazines, and in a book on the Gulf war.

Related Works and Resources

Since its publication, *Ulysses* has been the subject of study, analysis, interpretation, criticism, adulation, and mockery, and its impact runs the spectrum from high to low culture. Works that have been inspired by *Ulysses*—and for that matter, by much of the Joycean oeuvre—can be found in many mediums. Following are representative adaptations of Joyce's work in various forms, as well as resources for further information, celebration, and study.

NOVELS

Gilligan's Wake, by Tom Carson (Picador, 2003). A loose parody of Joyce that simultaneously tells the individual stories of the characters on the famous television show *Gilligan's Island*.

The House on Eccles Road, by Judith Kitchen (Graywolf Press, 2002). Details the events of June 16, 1999, in Dublin, Ohio, from the perspective of Molly, a fifty-one-year-old American woman who is married to an introverted Leo.

Murder in the Latin Quarter, by Tony Hays (Iris Press, 1993). In Paris, Joyce and his fellow expats meet in this murder mystery.

The Life of Leopold Bloom: A Novel, by Peter Costello (Roberts Rinehart, 1992). Costello reconstructs Bloom's life up to June 16, 1904, and speculates as to the rest. Interlaced with momentous events in Ireland during this period.

Masks of the Illuminati, by Robert Anton Wilson (Dell, 1990). The two main characters are Albert Einstein and James Joyce, who meet in a pub in Switzerland and together embark on a journey.

The Dalkey Archive, by Flann O'Brien (Dalkey Archive Press, 1964). This Irish writer's witty comic fantasy is a study in derision. Joyce's life and work are two of O'Brien's many targets.

FILMS

Bl..m, 2003. Directed by Sean Walsh and starring Stephen Rea. This recent film version of *Ulysses* has received widespread critical acclaim as a cleverly structured and interwoven adaptation of the novel that is faithful to *Ulysses'* modernist spirit.

Bloomsday Cabaret, 2004. Directed by Rosemary House. Tells the story of music in the life and literature of James Joyce against a Canadian Bloomsday backdrop. The film documents three Canadian Joyce enthusiasts on a pilgrimage to Dublin while interspersing glimpses of Canada's own Joycean celebrations and obsessions.

The Dead, 1987. Directed by John Huston. In his last film, Huston directs his daughter, Angelica Huston, in this version of Joyce's short story. The critic Hal Hinson wrote, "Watching it, you're momentarily swept away, and the experience—like the experience of anything great in art—is rapturous, consuming, sublime."

Famous Author Series: James Joyce, 1996. Documentary.

Finnegans Wake, 1967. Directed by Mary Ellen Bute and starring Martin J. Kelley. Currently there are no copies of this film on VHS or DVD, but 16 mm copies are available at some museums and Joycean institutions. In his review of the film, Leonard Maltin wrote, "James Joyce's classic story of an Irish tavern-keeper who dreams of attending his own wake is brought to the screen with great energy and control."

Is There One Who Understands Me?: The World of James Joyce, 1982. Directed by Shep Morgan and Sean O'Mordha. A feature-length biographical documentary that is an accessible introduction to Joyce's life and works. This artistic film mixes present-day shots of Paris and Dublin with those of Joyce's time, and includes interviews with Joycean scholars such as Richard Ellmann.

James Joyce: The Trials of Ulysses, 2000. Directed by Ian Graham. The film recounts the book's early battles against charges of obscenity, and Joyce's struggle to get the book published. There is an emphasis on Joyce's relationship with Nora.

James Joyce's Women, 1985. Directed by Michael Pearce and starring Fionnula Flanagan. Set at the beginning of the twentieth century, and based on some of Joyce's most controversial passages, the film depicts the writer's intimate relationships with the key women in his life: wife, benefactress, and publisher, as well as dramatizing three of his female characters. Originally a play.

Joyce in June, 1982. TV movie directed by Donald McWhinnie and starring Stephen Rea and Gabriel Byrne.

Joyce to the World (not yet released). Directed, produced, and edited by Fritzi Horstman (Diana J. Wynne, producer and writer). This feature-length documentary seeks to explain the phenomenon of Bloomsday. It also provides extensive historic and biographical background, affirming Joyce's place in literature and Ireland as a brilliant, irreverent emissary of a rich cultural tradition.

Leo, 2002. Directed by Mehdi Norowzian and starring Joseph Fiennes, Elizabeth Shue, Sam Shepard, and Dennis Hopper. Inspired by Joyce's characters, this story is set in the American South. Though the film contains references to *Ulysses* and explores a few of the same themes, it is not by any means intended as a faithful retelling of the story.

Les Exilés, 1975. Directed by Guy Lessertisseur. Based on Joyce's play.

Nora, 2000. Directed by Pat Murphy, starring Ewan McGregor and Susan Lynch. Based on the biography by Brenda Maddox, *Nora* is a fictional film set in 1904 about Joyce's wife and muse. The film is an attempt to demystify Joyce and understand Nora, the most important person in his life.

A Portrait of the Artist as a Young Man, 1977. Directed by Joseph Strick. Another adaptation of Joyce's work in the hands of Strick, a decade after his *Ulysses*, this time starring Bosco Hogan. The dialogue is largely taken from Joyce's text.

The Producers, 1968. Directed by Mel Brooks. This popular comedy contains a character named Leo Bloom.

A Shout from the Streets, 2000. Directed by Fred DeVecca. A short film inspired by *Ulysses*.

10 Great Writers, Vol. 7: James Joyce, 1988. Documentary.

Uliisses, 1982 (West Germany). Directed by Werner Nekes. An experimental film about the history of cinema filtered through Homer and Joyce.

Ulysses, 1967. Directed by Joseph Strick and starring Milo O'Shea. This film was the first substantial attempt at a cinematic adaptation of Joyce's novel, and fittingly, it was quite controversial. Strick sets *Ulysses* in the Dublin of the 1960s, complete with electricity and period fashion.

The Wake, 2000 (Denmark). Directed by Michael Kvium and Christian Lemmerz. This silent film takes its title and motives from *Finnegans Wake*.

Plays

James Joyce's The Dead is a musical conceived by Richard Nelson, with music by Shaun Davey, that opened in 1999, starring Christopher Walken as Gabriel Conroy. A retelling of Joyce's famous short story about a Christmastime gathering in Dublin, the play was a popular success and won a Tony Award for Best Book.

Mr. Joyce Is Leaving Paris, by Tom Gallacher, is a drama concerning Joyce's last days in Paris in 1939, in which he goes through a crisis like Stephen's in *Ulysses*. Published by Calder and Boyars.

Molly Bloom is the creation of singer Anna Zapparoli and her husband, composer Mario Borciani. It is a jazz/cabaret–style musical taking Molly's soliloquy as its inspiration. Opened in 2000 at the Edinburgh Fringe Festival to the dismay of Stephen Joyce, James Joyce's grandson.

Travesties, a play by Tom Stoppard, is situated in Switzerland in 1917, with James Joyce, Lenin, and Tristan Tzara as characters who are each wrestling with their respective revolutions: literary, political, and artistic.

Ulysses in Nighttown, a dramatization by Marjorie Barkentin of Leopold Bloom's odyssey through the streets of Dublin directed by Burgess Meredith and starring Fionnula Flanagan. Performed in 1974 and was nominated for six Tony Awards including Best Play.

Music

SAMUEL BARBER, "Secrets of the Old." Between 1935 and 1972, Barber composed pieces based on material taken from *Chamber Music*, *Finnegans Wake*, and *Ulysses*, available on this two-disc set.

KATE BUSH, "The Sensual World," 1989. The lyrics from this song are adapted from Molly's soliloquy in *Ulysses*.

JOHN CAGE, "The Wonderful Widow of Eighteen Springs"; "Roaratorio"; "An Alphabet"; and "Nowth Upon Nacht," composed between 1942 and 1984. All pieces inspired from Joyce's texts. "Roaratorio" specifically incorporates phrases from *Finnegans Wake* into a tapestry of noise, voice, song, and Irish traditional music.

THE JAMES JOYCE CENTRE IN DUBLIN produced a compilation of music in 2003 called "Classical Ulysses," which features pieces in the order of their appearances in the text. On June 16, 1904, Leopold Bloom encountered live music by Mozart, Gounod, Mendelssohn, Handel, Liszt, Bellini, Rosetti, and Verdi.

JEFFERSON AIRPLANE, "rejoyce," 1967. The lyrics of this song are a stream-of-consciousness exploration around themes and characters taken from *Ulysses*.

ELIZABETH LAUER, "Seven Songs on Poems of James Joyce," 1955. Poems from *Chamber Music* are performed by the mezzo-soprano, accompanied by piano.

GERARD VICTORY, "Five Songs of James Joyce," 1978; "Six Epiphanies of the Author: A Symphonic Study in Memory of James Joyce," 1981.

VISUAL ARTS

Various works by: William Anastasi, Peter Bailey, Constantin Brancusi, Ian Breakwell, John Christie, Nick Cudworth, John Furnival, Richard Hamilton, Keith Hardwick, Patrick Ireland, Ciaran Lennon, Henri Matisse, Robert Motherwell, Bernard Moxham, Megan O'Beirne, Seamus O'Brien, Tom Phillips, Kathy Prendergast, Man Ray, Noel Sheridan, Tony Smith, Rey Tanaka, Karl Torok, Shaun Walsh, Steve Williams.

Ear's Eye for James Joyce, an artist's book by Susan Weil. Weil has been making art inspired by the texts of James Joyce since 1985. She paints, draws, etches, collages, cuts, and does handwork, all in a tribute to Joyce.

The Ulysses Suite, by Paul Joyce. A man who calls himself James Joyce's great-grandnephew has recently completed a series of eighteen oil paintings and etchings that were inspired by each of the eighteen chapters of *Ulysses*.

NONFICTION BOOKS

Lucia Joyce: To Dance in the Wake, by Carol Loeb Shloss (Farrar Straus & Giroux, 2003). Shloss's book deviates from other studies about Lucia and offers new analyses of Joyce's life, and presents his daughter as a collaborator in his artistic process.

James Joyce: A Literary Reference, by Nicholas Fargnoli, editor (Carroll & Graf Publishers, 2003). Fargnoli charts the trajectory of *Ulysses* from publication to entry into the modern literary canon with a collection of tributes, correspondence, excerpts from book reviews, photographs, and reminiscences.

Re Joyce, by Anthony Burgess (W.W. Norton, 1968, 2000). A celebration of and an introductory guide to *Ulysses* and *Finnegans Wake*. According to Burgess, *ReJoyce* "does not pretend to scholarship, only a desire to help the average reader who wants to know Joyce's work but has been scared off by the professors." Burgess writes passionately and wittily about Joyce's revolutionary use of language.

Nora: The Real Life of Molly Bloom, by Brenda Maddox (Houghton Mifflin, 1988, 2000). This book gives weight to the theory that Nora was the inspiration for *Ulysses'* Molly Bloom, *Finnegans Wake*'s Anna Livia Plurabelle, and principal females in all his other writings. Well written and full of little-known facts about Joyce, Nora, and their relationship.

The Years of Bloom: James Joyce in Trieste, 1904–1920, by John McCourt (University of Wisconsin Press, 2000). This book focuses on how Joyce's time in Trieste influenced him as an author and as a man. McCourt has a profound understanding of the culture and inhabitants of Trieste, and the book is meticulously researched.

The Cast of Characters: A Reading of Ulysses, by Paul Schwaber (Yale University Press, 1999). This book is an attempt at psychoanalysis of the main characters in *Ulysses*, which reveals their complex and rich inner lives.

The New Bloomsday Book (3rd edition), by Harry Blamires (Routledge Press, 1996). This is a simple and useful guide to Joyce's text, in which each chapter corresponds to a chapter in *Ulysses*. It summarizes and clarifies the work, while highlighting the important themes.

Joyce and the Jews: Culture and Texts, by Ira Nadel (University Press of Florida, 1995). Nadel pieces together the complicated biographical and cultural elements of Joyce's affinity with the Jews.

The Irish Ulysses, by Maria Tymoczko (University of California Press, 1994). Tymoczko challenges the conventional view that Joyce rejected Irish literature, and demonstrates how Irish writing, culture, and imagery greatly influenced his work.

The Scandal of Ulysses: The Sensational Life of a Twentieth-Century Masterpiece, by Bruce Arnold (St. Martin's Press, 1992). Arnold traces the complex publishing history of *Ulysses*, starting with the 1922 Shakespeare and Company edition and ending with Gabler's controversial 1986 edition, which incensed many Joyceans.

Ulysses Annotated, by Don Gifford and Robert J. Seidman (University of California Press, 1989). An enormous book that attempts to annotate every intertextual reference and narrative device used by Joyce. Robert N. Ross, of the *Western Humanities Review*, writes that this book "teaches more than how to read a particular novel; it teaches us more profoundly how to read anything. This, I think, is the book's main virtue. It teaches us readers how to transform the brute fact of our world."

Ulysses, by Hugh Kenner (Johns Hopkins University Press, 1987). A study of Joyce as a modernist. This book traces his development as a writer and his place in the modernist era. It also focuses on the structure of *Ulysses*, giving weight to the Homeric parallels and stylistic choices.

Ulysses—Modern Critical Interpretations, Harold Bloom, editor (Chelsea House, 1987, 2003). A collection of critical essays on *Ulysses* published during the second half of the twentieth century.

Allusions in Ulysses, by Weldon Thornton (University of North Carolina Press, 1982). Similar in structure to *Ulysses Annotated*, this guide is a page-by-page list of Joycean allusions, classical and otherwise.

James Joyce's Ulysses: Critical Essays, Clive Hart and David Hayman, editors (University of California Press, 1977). This book contains eighteen original essays by leading Joyce scholars on the eighteen chapters of *Ulysses*.

Ulysses on the Liffey, by Richard Ellmann (Oxford University Press, 1973). Ellmann, one of the most respected and accomplished Joyce scholars, has a comprehensive understanding of Joyce, and his writing is clear and concise. This is a good companion to his canonical book on Joyce's life.

James Joyce's Ulysses, by Stuart Gilbert (Vintage Books, 1955; originally published in 1932). The first book-length study of *Ulysses*, this book became influential as Gilbert presented the significance of the Homeric framework.

Websites (selected)

http://www.as.miami.edu/english/jjls/jjls.htm

http://www.bibliomania.com

http://english.ohio-state.edu/organizations/ijjf

http://www.jamesjoyce.ie

http://www.jamesjoycehouse.com

http://www.jjoycebiblio.org

http://www.joycean.org

http://www.joycefoundation.ch

http://joycesociety.org

http://publish.uwo.ca/~mgroden/flying1.html

http://www.themodernword.com/joyce

http://www.utexas.edu/utpress/journals/jjsa.html

http://www.utulsa.edu/jjoyceqtrly

http://www.2street.com/joyce

http://www.visitdublin.com

PILGRIMAGE SITES

The James Joyce Centre in Dublin, 35 North Great Georges Street, Dublin 1, Ireland. Among other things, organizes the annual Bloomsday celebration in Dublin. The center has a collection of *Ulysses*- and Joyce-related memorabilia, such as the door to number 7 Eccles Street, and a library of Joyce works, translations, and criticism. The center offers walking tours that highlight Joycean landmarks. One can purchase a *Ulysses* map of Dublin for one euro at the center that details Bloom's path.

Joyce Tower and Museum, Sandycove, County Dublin, Ireland. The Joyce Tower was one of a series of Martello towers built to withstand an invasion by Napoleon and now holds a museum devoted to the life and works of James Joyce, who made the tower, nine miles south of Dublin, the setting for the first chapter of *Ulysses*.

Trieste, Italy, was Joyce's home for sixteen years after leaving Dublin. One can visit 30 via San Nicolo, the building where Joyce and his family lived in a small room without cooking facilities.

Shakespeare and Company, 37 rue de la Bucherie, Paris, France (www.shakespeareco.org). The famous bookstore founded by Sylvia Beach that published the first edition of *Ulysses*.

CITIES WITH BLOOMSDAY CELEBRATIONS (SELECTED)

U.S.

ALASKA
Anchorage

ARIZONA
Phoenix

CALIFORNIA
Berkeley
Sacramento
San Diego
San Francisco

FLORIDA
Palm Beach
Sarasota

ILLINOIS
Champaign-Urbana
Chicago

MARYLAND
Baltimore

MASSACHUSETTS
Boston
Dedham
Martha's Vineyard

MISSOURI
Kansas City

NEW YORK
Buffalo
New York (*Bloomsday on Broadway*)
Syracuse

OHIO
Cincinnati

PENNSYLVANIA
Philadelphia

WASHINGTON
Seattle
Spokane

OUTSIDE U.S.

ARGENTINA
Buenos Aires

AUSTRALIA
Melbourne
Sydney

CANADA
Toronto

ENGLAND
London

FRANCE
Paris

IRELAND
Dublin

JAPAN
Tokyo

MEXICO
Mexico City

NEW ZEALAND
Auckland

NORWAY
Eidsvoll

SCOTLAND
Glasgow

SWITZERLAND
Zurich

MISCELLANEA

Traveling at 60 mph, you can drive from New York to Los Angeles in the time it takes to listen to *Ulysses* on tape.

In recent years, the number of Bloomsday celebrations worldwide has approached two hundred, in sixty different countries.

In 1993, Joyce's likeness appeared on the front of the Irish ten-pound note. On the back was the opening paragraph of *Finnegans Wake*.

In Dedham, Massachusetts, the "James Joyce Ramble," a 10K race to celebrate Joyce has been going strong since 1984, and actors in period garb read *Ulysses* aloud at various points along the 6.2-mile course through the center of town, cheering on approximately three thousand runners.

In 1912, Joyce opened the Volta Theatre, the first Irish cinema in Dublin, a short-lived business adventure.

It's been said that Joyce based Bloom on an acquaintance named Alfred H. Hunter, who took care of Joyce after he'd been knocked down in a fight.

Stephen Dedalus was a pseudonym under which Joyce published several stories before *Portrait of the Artist as a Young Man*.

In 2002, Molly, Leopold, and Stephen Dedalus ranked number eight, four, and nine respectively on *Book Magazine*'s list of the "100 Best Characters in Fiction Since 1900."

On A&E's "1000 Most Important People of the Millennium," Joyce weighed in at number eighty six.

The Modern Library named *Ulysses* number one on its list of the "Top 100 Titles of the Century," a list that also includes *Finnegans Wake* and *A Portrait of the Artist as a Young Man*.

INSTITUTIONS AND PUBLICATIONS

The James Joyce Centre
35 North Great Georges Street
Dublin 1
Ireland

Phone: (+353) 1-878-8547
Fax: (+353) 1-878-8488
info@jamesjoyce.ie
www.jamesjoyce.ie

The International James Joyce Foundation
Department of English
The Ohio State University
164 West 17th Avenue
Columbus, Ohio 43210

Phone: (614) 292-2061
Fax: (614) 292-7816
ijjf@osu.edu
www.cohums.ohio-state.edu/english/organizations/ijjf/main/htm

Joyce Studies Annual
P. O. Box 7819
University of Texas Press
Austin, Texas 78713
Phone: (512) 232-7621
Fax: (512) 471-9646

journals@uts.cc.utexas.edu
www.utexas.edu/depts/utpress/journals/jjca.html

James Joyce Literary Supplement
Department of English
Box 248145
University of Miami
Coral Gables, Florida 33124

Phone: (305) 284-3140
jjls.english@miami.edu
www.as.miami.edu/english/jjls/jjls.htm

James Joyce Quarterly
University of Tulsa
600 South College Avenue
Tulsa, Oklahoma 74104-3189

Phone: (918) 631-2501
Fax: (918) 584-0623
www.utulsa.edu/jjoyceqtrly/homejjq.html

The James Joyce Society
Nick Fargnoli, President
Meetings held at: Gotham Book Mart
41 West 47th Street
New York, New York 10036

Phone: (516) 764-3119
info@joycesociety.org
www.joycesociety.org

James Joyce Foundation
P.O. Box 1250
Rozelle NSW 2039

Australia

Phone: (+61) (0)2-9555-2540
Fax: (+61) (0)2-9555-9250
ozbloom@enternet.com.au

The James Joyce Summer School
Anne Fogarty, Director
School of English
University College, Dublin
Belfield
Dublin 4
Ireland

anne.fogarty@ucd.ie
www.artsworld.ie/joyce_school

Zürich James Joyce Foundation
Augustinergasse 9
CH-8001 Zürich
Switzerland

Phone: (+41) 1-2118301
Fax: (+41) 1-2125128
joyce@es.unizh.ch
www.joycefoundation.ch

Bibliography

Barnes, Djuna, "James Joyce." *Vanity Fair* (April 1922): 65, 104.

Beach, Sylvia, *Shakespeare and Company* (Lincoln: University of Nebraska Press, 1959; New York: Harcourt Brace & Company, 1991).

Beja, Morris, *James Joyce: A Literary Life* (Columbus: Ohio State University Press, 1992).

Bloom, Harold (ed.), *James Joyce: Modern Critical Views* (New York and Philadelphia: Chelsea House, 1986).

Cowley, Malcolm, *Writers at Work: Paris Review Interviews* (New York: Viking Press, 1959).

Coyle, John (ed.), *James Joyce: Ulysses, Portrait of the Artist as a Young Man* (New York: Columbia University Press, 1998).

Davies, Stan Gébler, *James Joyce: A Portrait of the Artist* (New York: Stein and Day, 1975).

Deming, Robert H. (ed.), *James Joyce: The Critical Heritage, Volume One 1902–1927* (New York: Barnes & Noble, 1970).

Deming, Robert H. (ed.), *James Joyce: The Critical Heritage, Volume Two 1928–1941* (New York: Barnes & Noble, 1970).

Ellmann, Richard, *James Joyce* (New York: Oxford University Press, 1959, 1982).

Ellmann, Richard, *Selected Letters of James Joyce* (New York: Viking Press, 1957, 1966, 1975).

Forster, E. M., *Aspects of the Novel* (San Diego, New York, London: Harvest, HBJ, 1927).

Gilbert, Stuart (ed.), *Letters of James Joyce* (New York: Viking Press, 1966).

Gorman, Herbert, *James Joyce* (New York: Octagon/Farrar Straus & Giroux, 1974).

Johnson, Paul, *Modern Times: The World from the Twenties to the Eighties* (New York: Harper & Row, 1983).

Joyce, Stanislaus, *Recollections of James Joyce*, trans. Ellsworth Mason (New York: James Joyce Society, 1950).

Mason, Ellsworth, and Richard Ellmann (eds.) *The Critical Writings of James Joyce* (New York: Viking Press, 1959).

Miller, Henry, *The Cosmological Eye* (New York: New Directions, 1939).

Nabokov, Vladimir, *Lectures on Literature*, ed. Fredson Bowers (San Diego, New York, London: Harvest, HBJ, 1927).

Noble, Joan Russell, *Recollections of Virginia Woolf* (New York: William Morrow and Company, 1972).

O'Brien, Edna, *James Joyce* (New York: Viking Penguin, 1999).

Potts, Willard (ed.), *Portraits of the Artist in Exile* (Seattle and London: University of Washington Press, 1979).

Pound, Ezra, *Literary Essays of Ezra Pound*, ed. T. S. Eliot (New York: New Directions, 1918, 1920, 1935).

Pound, Ezra, "*Paris Letter*." The Dial (June 1922): 626.

Read, Forrest (ed.), *Pound/Joyce: Letters and Essays* (New York: New Directions, 1967).

Wilson, Edmund, *Axel's Castle: A Study of the Imaginative Literature of 1870–1930* (New York: Charles Scribner's Sons, 1931).

Wilson, Edmund, "Ulysses." *The New Republic* (July 1922): 164-166.

Acknowledgments

I am grateful to the following people for their inspired work:

Mary Gordon, to whom I'm indebted for her eloquent essay and for her intelligence, generosity, and grace. To Dan Tucker, for his ideas, his thoughtfulness, and his indefatigable sense of humor. To Elizabeth Zimmermann, for her elegant design and attention to detail; and Elizabeth Johnson, for her care and diligence.

My gratitude to Robert Spoo for his literary and legal insights, Jin Di for his reflections on translating Ulysses, Mike Barsanti for his knowledge of the Ulysses manuscript, and Lettie Teague for taking a small detail and creating a lively piece of writing. To all of these people, my thanks for their generosity.

For the colorful contributions of the "Bloomsday on Broadway" participants and to the generous people at the Bloomsday centers around the world—many thanks.

Among the individuals and institutions to whom I am grateful for their assistance with research and for providing written and photographic material: Helen Monaghan, director of the James Joyce Centre; Robert Nicholson, curator of the Joyce Museum in Sandycove; Senator David Norris; Luca Crispi; Katherine McSharry at the National Library of Ireland; Richard Reyes-Gavilan and the helpful staff at the New York Public Library; Sam Slote at SUNY Buffalo; Caraid O'Brien, Cathy Minton, and the staff of Symphony Space; Frances Devlin-Glass; Margaret Gibson Harmsworth; Guy Davenport; and Jenny Finegan of Dublin Tourism.

Thanks to my parents, Gay and Tom, and my brother, Andrew, for their careful readings of the manuscript, and for their enthusiasm; to

Warner Dick for his meticulous help; and to Daniel Kunitz for reading sections of the book in the early stages.

And my gratitude to Vintage Books: to LuAnn Walther, John Siciliano, Barbara Richard, Cathy Aison, Russell Perreault, Jennifer Marshall, and all the people there who participated in *yes I said yes I will Yes*.

Photo Permissions

Cover illustration, "James Joyce at Midnight," drawing by Desmond Harmsworth, by permission of Harry Ransom Humanities Research Center, The University of Texas at Austin, and Mme. Margaret Gibson Harmsworth.

pp. IV-V Courtesy of the Dublin Tourism Centre, www.visitdublin.com.

pp. 18, 22, 25, 40, 51 Poetry/Rare Books Collection, University Libraries, University at Buffalo, The State University of New York.

p. 31 Special Collections Research Center, Morris Library, Southern Illinois University at Carbondale.

p. 38 Photograph by C. P. Curran © Elizabeth Solterer; reproduced by permission of University College Dublin Library.

p. 44 John Quinn Papers, Manuscripts and Archives Division, The New York Public Library, Astor, Lenox and Tilden Foundations.

p. 48 © Berenice Abbott/Commerce Graphics Ltd., Inc., New York.

p. 52 Drawing by F. Scott Fitzgerald, reproduced by permission of the Harold Ober Associates. Image source: *Shakespeare and Company* by Sylvia Beach (Lincoln: University of Nebraska Press, 1980, 1991. Harcourt Brace & Company, New York, 1959).

p. 55 © Horst Tappe.

p. 56 © Rosenbach Museum and Library, Philadelphia.

p. 59 "Joyce's sketch of Bloom," reproduced by permission of Charles Deering McCormick Library of Special Collections, Northwestern University Library.

p. 62 © Getty Images.

p. 69 Courtesy of Random House, Inc.

p. 70 Photograph by Philip Massey © The James Joyce Centre, Dublin.

p. 73 © The James Joyce Centre, Dublin.

p. 84 © Bloomsday in Melbourne Inc.

p. 89 Photograph by Lionel Simmons, Toronto.

p. 90 Photograph by Carola Giedion-Welcker, © Zurich James Joyce Foundation.

p. 94 © Guy Davenport.

Text Permissions

Particulars of punctuation, spelling, and style have been preserved as they appear in the original sources.

"Obituary of James Joyce" reprinted courtesy of the *Irish Independent* (pages 54-5).

Paul Léon excerpts are from *Portraits of the Artist in Exile: Recollections of James Joyce by Europeans* (University of Washington Press, 1979). Reprinted by permission of the University of Washington Press.

Edna O'Brien excerpts from *James Joyce* by Edna O'Brien, © 1999 by Edna O'Brien. Used by permission of Viking Penguin, a division of Penguin Group (USA) Inc.

Bernard Shaw, "Extract from a letter to Sylvia Beach (11 June 1921)," reprinted courtesy of The Society of Authors, on behalf of the Bernard Shaw Estate (page 35).

Philippe Soupault excerpts are from *Portraits of the Artist in Exile: Recollections of James Joyce by Europeans* (University of Washington Press, 1979). Reprinted by permission of the University of Washington Press.

Tennessee Williams, "A Report on Four Writers of the Modern Psychological School," © 2003 by The University of the South. Excerpt reprinted by permission of Georges Borchardt, Inc. for the Tennessee Williams Estate, and courtesy Harry Ransom Humanities Research Center, The University of Texas at Austin (pages 64-5).

Edmund Wilson, excerpts from "James Joyce" from *Axel's Castle: A Study in the Imaginative Literature of 1870–1930* by Edmund Wilson, © 1931 by Charles Scribner's Sons. Copyright renewed 1958 by Edmund Wilson. Reprinted by permission of Farrar, Straus and Giroux, LLC.

Index

Page numbers set in *italics* indicate illustrations. Names set in *italics* refer to characters from Joyce's fiction.

BY JAMES JOYCE

ULYSSES

"Ulysses *will immortalize its author with the same certainty that* Gargantua *immortalized Rabelais, and* The Brothers Karamazov *immortalized Dostoevsky. . . . It comes nearer to being the perfect revelation of a personality than any book in existence.*" —The New York Times

The most famous day in literature is June 16, 1904, when a certain Mr. Leopold Bloom of Dublin eats a kidney for breakfast, attends a funeral, admires a girl on the beach, contemplates his wife's imminent adultery, and, late at night, befriends a drunken young poet in the city's red-light district. An earthy story, a virtuoso technical display, and a literary revolution all rolled into one, James Joyce's *Ulysses* is a touchstone of our modernity and one of the towering achievements of the human mind.

This revised volume follows the complete unabridged text as corrected in 1961. It contains the original foreword by the author and the historic court ruling to remove the federal ban. It also contains page references to the first American edition of 1934.

Fiction/Literature/0-679-72276-9

DUBLINERS

With these fifteen stories James Joyce reinvented the art of fiction, using a scrupulous, deadpan realism to convey truths that were at once blasphemous and sacramental. Whether writing about the death of a fallen priest, the petty sexual and fiscal machinations of "Two Gallants," or of the Christmas party at which an uprooted intellectual discovers just how little he really knows about his wife, Joyce takes narrative to places it had never been before.

Fiction/Literature/0-679-73990-4

A PORTRAIT OF THE ARTIST AS A YOUNG MAN

James Joyce's supremely innovative fictional autobiography is also, in the apt phrase of the biographer Richard Ellmann, nothing less than "the gestation of a soul." For as he describes the shabby, cloying, and sometimes terrifying Dublin upbringing of his alter ego, Stephen Dedalus, Joyce immerses the reader in his emerging consciousness, employing language that ranges from baby talk to hellfire sermon to a triumphant artist's manifesto. The result is a novel of immense boldness, eloquence, and energy, a work that inaugurated a literary revolution and has become a model for the portrayal of the self in our time.

Fiction/Literature/0-679-73989-0

VINTAGE INTERNATIONAL
Available at your local bookstore, or call toll-free to order:
1-800-793-2665 (credit cards only)